D0254565

ALBRIGHT COLLEGE
LIBRARY

PRESENTED BY
National Council of American-Soviet Friendship, Inc.

SOVIET DEMOCRACY
and how it works

by JESSICA SMITH

Cover designed by Ernest Socolov
All photos from Sovfoto

Reprinted, with additions,
From *New World Review*,
Jan.-July, 1967

Published by

NATIONAL COUNCIL OF
AMERICAN-SOVIET FRIENDSHIP

Suite 304, 156 Fifth Avenue
New York, N. Y. 10010
1969

947
S651s

116300

TABLE OF CONTENTS

Introduction 5

Chapter 1: USSR Government Structure 7

Chapter 2: The Local Soviets 18

Chapter 3: City Soviets in Irkutsk and Kiev 28

Chapter 4: A District Soviet in Moscow 38

Chapter 5: Others' Impressions—New Measures 59

Chapter 6: The Rural Soviets 65

Chapter 7: New Data on the Rural Soviets 73

The Soviet of the Village Novozhivotinnoye
on the Don, *by Ivan Kovalkin* 93

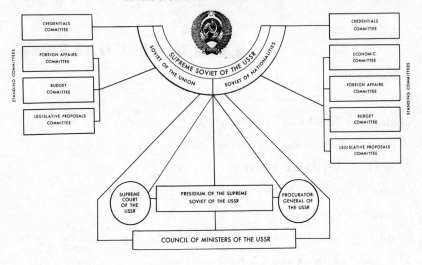

About the Author

Jessica Smith is the editor of *New World Review*. She is a lifetime student of the Soviet Union, having spent five years altogether in that country. Her seventh visit was in the summer of 1967. She is the author of *Women in Soviet Russia* and *People Come First* and numerous pamphlets and articles on the USSR and American-Soviet relations and peace issues. She has worked closely with the National Council of American-Soviet Friendship since its inception, as a member of its Board of Directors.

4

Introduction

WE ARE offering this reprint of a series of articles on Soviet democracy, originally published in *New World Review*, with some added up-to-date material, because so many questions are directed both to the National Council of American-Soviet Friendship and *New World Review* on the question of democracy in the Soviet Union.

This material does not pretend to cover the whole field of Soviet democracy. A complete picture would require examining this question in connection with every area of Soviet life.

It does, however, take hold of the question at the most decisive point—covering the Soviet system of government and how it works, especially in the primary organs of state power. The local Soviets are the vehicle through which the whole people of all the 100 nationalities which make up the Soviet state, living in its fifteen Union republics and their numerous autonomous republics and regions, participate in the running of the state and in making the decisions in the matters that affect their daily lives most closely.

We believe this pamphlet contains material not sufficiently known to the American public generally. Years of anti-Soviet propaganda have left a widespread impression of government by edict and a rubber stamp parliament, which should be corrected by the facts in this pamphlet.

Too often, as well, judgments about the Soviet Union are reached on the basis of isolated instances of trials of writers and others for anti-Soviet activities, cited as proof that the unjustified persecutions of the Stalin era are still continuing.

But we are deeply convinced that the mass repressions of the Stalin period are a thing of the past and can never return in the mature socialist society the Soviet Union has established in its over fifty years of experience.

With certain ups and downs resulting mainly from external causes, Soviet society has become more free and flexible today than ever before. Matters once taboo are now discussed fully and openly.

The economic reform is affecting all areas of Soviet life, and has led in recent months to an extension of the rights and responsibilities

5

of the local Soviets in the sphere of economic activities, opening up new resources for them in the work of improving the well-being of the people, with the direct participation of the people themselves.

The economic reform is also reflected in expanding trade-union democracy, with the workers participating more closely than ever in problems of management of industry, through the widespread production conferences, and sharing directly in the distribution of the profits accruing through more efficient management which go to no individual, but mean better housing and social and cultural amenities and bonuses for workers' higher production.

In science, the days of political dictation, as in the days when Lysenko ruled the roost in genetics, are gone forever and there is full freedom for experimentation, the struggle of opposing ideas, bold new solutions. Here is the way this was expressed by Academician Stanislav Strumilin, one of the USSR's leading economists:

> Divergences of opinion in scientific discussions no longer frighten us, and that is a good thing. In free debate ideas that have outlived their time gradually fall away like dead leaves in autumn. New, creative ideas are tested and generalized in a clash of the best minds, and scientific life flourishes. When such an atmosphere is created, even experienced, inveterate dogmatists seem to be infected by the creative spirit and awaken from their long sleep. Even old mold produces penicillin.
> *From an article in* Komsomolskaya Pravda, *February 16, 1968*

And the world-renowned Soviet physicist, Academician Peter Kapitsa, declared:

> . . . an authoritative and healthy public opinion can be created only in an atmosphere of lively and active thought, in an atmosphere of quest and productive creation. An absolute condition for such an atmosphere is the clash of differing opinions, the exchange of debatable ideas, discussions and disputes. In recent years we've made a colossal step forward in that direction. Yet we still conduct discussions poorly, with insufficient skill and knowledge . . .
> Discussion is dialectics itself. It is in the conflict of opposites that truth is born. . . . It is absolutely obvious that the clash of different styles, manners, and creative credos is just as useful for the development of art as is the conflict of opinions for progress in science. Society gains from polemics and from the frank exchange of opinions. This has been demonstrated once again by the economics discussion in our press, which played a useful role in preparing the party's decision on rebuilding the planning and guidance of industry.
> *From an interview published in* Yunost (*Youth magazine*), *#1, 1967.*

This, we believe, is the direction in which Soviet society is moving.

J. S.

6

Chapter 1

USSR GOVERNMENT STRUCTURE

IT IS common practice in our country to describe the Soviet Union as a "totalitarian" state, meaning that everything is decided at the top and that the people in general have practically nothing to say. Most Americans dismiss the idea that there is or can be such a thing as Soviet democracy. Since in Soviet elections there is only one candidate on the ballot, without even a write-in provision, they conclude that the voters really have no choice. They consider that when over 99 per cent of the people turn out to vote this only shows that the whole thing is a farce, that the people simply flock to the polls like sheep and vote as they are told. The general impression is that the USSR Supreme Soviet is just a rubber stamp for decisions already made by Soviet Party and Government leaders.

There is no simple answer to these questions for Americans, whose traditions and procedures are so different. It is necessary to examine the whole process of government in the Soviet Union from top to bottom and to see how it functions from day to day. Only in this way is it possible to understand the great and growing participation of the Soviet people in deciding the questions which affect their daily lives, even though admittedly many shortcomings still exist.

One hears and reads a great deal in the Soviet Union about the constant growth of Soviet democracy through people's participation in government, through the extension of people's self-government, and through the gradual taking over of actual functions of government by organizations of the people.

On my visits in 1961, 1964 and 1967, I have made a special effort to see how this people's participation in government works out at the point where it is most highly developed and most effective—the local Soviets.

Government Structure and Elections

IT IS by studying these primary organs that the way the Soviet Government operates can best be understood. I shall begin by sketching the structure of government as a whole briefly, to show how the local Soviets fit in.

The Supreme Soviet of the USSR, the Soviet Parliament, is the highest organ of Soviet power. It holds legislative power for the country as a whole, represents the USSR in international relations, is responsible for all questions of war and peace. It is important to insert a word about the role of the Communist Party at this point, since there is an impression that all laws and policies emanate from the Communist Party alone, through its Presidium, plenary sessions and its Central Committee and its National Congresses. There is of course no gainsaying the leading role of the Party, and its determining role in legislation on domestic and foreign policies. But in matters of state concern, the Party never acts alone. Most important decrees and decisions on internal state matters are issued jointly by the Party and the Government.

It should be clearly understood that only the Supreme Soviet of the USSR is empowered to make the country's laws.

Some legislation, especially on such vital matters as the successive economic plans and the recent changes in economic management, is first considered at a plenary session of the Central Committee or full Congress of the CPSU. What is there agreed upon, while embodying basic policies, can, however, be no more than a draft as far as the required legislation is concerned. This is then submitted for public discussion on the one hand, and for careful working over by the legislative commission of the Supreme Soviet, taking the views of the public into account, before a final draft is submitted to a session of the Supreme Soviet for discussion and amendment by the deputies, after which it is enacted into law. In recent years there has been much more discussion on such matters than formerly at Supreme Soviet sessions and amendments to proposed legislation have become more frequent.

But a great deal of legislation is also initiated directly by the Supreme Soviet on the basis of proposals from its own members, the press, various organizations of the public, without prior submission of a draft by the CPSU. For the past several years, for example, the drafting of a new Soviet law on the family, which has been under wide public discussion for some time, has been in the hands of a commission of the Supreme Soviet of the USSR. The recent decree modifying divorce procedures, which will eventually be included in the final law, was a result of these discussions. [The new law was passed in 1968.]

The Supreme Soviet of the USSR is made up of two equal houses, the Soviet of the Union, elected from numerical constituencies throughout the country on the basis of one deputy per 300,000 people, and the Soviet of Nationalities, in which each Union Republic and national grouping has its own needs and interests represented. Irrespective of population, there are 32 seats for each of the fifteen Union Republics which make up the USSR; eleven for each Autonomous Republic, five for each autonomous region and one for each national area. (The number of deputies for each Union Republic was increased from 25 to 32 in 1966 to equalize the membership in

8

both houses, since the over-all increase in the Soviet population had meant an increase in the number of deputies to the Soviet of the Union.)

Both houses of the Supreme Soviet have equal powers in initiating legislation and all other matters, and all laws must be passed by both houses, a simple majority in each being required. Each house elects its own chairman. The chairmen of the two houses preside alternately at joint sessions.

The Supreme Soviet, at a joint session, elects a full time Presidium, which acts for it between sessions, and the President of the Presidium, who is formally the Soviet head of state. The Presidium has 33 members. Beside the Chairman, it has 15 Vice-Chairmen, one for each Union Republic, thus further insuring the role of the Union Republics in all state affairs. It also has a Secretary and 16 Members.

The Supreme Soviet, at a joint sitting, also elects the Chairman of the Council of Ministers of the USSR, equivalent to the Prime Minister, who draws up the list of ministers and submits it to the joint session for confirmation. The Supreme Soviet also elects the members of the Supreme Court of the USSR.

The Supreme Soviet normally holds sessions twice a year. Special sessions may be called at the discretion of the Presidium or on demand of any of the Union Republics.

Election Procedures

ELECTIONS to the Supreme Soviet must be held at least every four years. Everyone over the age of 18 has the right to vote, the only exceptions being those who have been declared legally insane or who are serving jail sentences. Any citizen who has reached the age of 18 may be elected to the lower Soviets and at 23 may be elected to the USSR Supreme Soviet. The age is 21 for election to a Union Republic Supreme Soviet. Elections to the Soviets at all levels are direct.

Soviet electoral law provides for several candidates being nominated and standing for election as deputies in each electoral district, although in practice only one candidate is in fact finally nominated in each constituency.

The right of nomination is vested in any organization or society, such as trade unions, Party or YCL, other youth organizations, state enterprises, cooperatives, cultural societies, military units, groups of workers, social organizations or meetings held in factories, collective and state farms or government institutions. Anyone may challenge or reject any name offered in nomination or offer another name.

In discussions I have held over many years I have always found the greatest difficulty in making any local Soviet official, Government or Party, understand our American attitude that there can be no real freedom of choice with only one candidate on the ballot. Only

9

on my most recent trip, in 1964, when I found a freer and more flexible attitude on all political questions than ever before and a readiness to discuss them without inhibitions, did I hear the question raised by various people of the desirability of having several candidates on the ballot.

In the *New York Times* of March 22, 1966, Peter Grose, the paper's Moscow correspondent, reported that Nagush K. Arutyunyan, Chairman of the Presidium of the Supreme Soviet of Armenia, had suggested that government elections might be more meaningful if there were more than one candidate for each place on the ballot. He raised the matter at the Armenian Party Congress held earlier in March in preparation for the 23rd CPSU Congress in Moscow. Noting the argument that there is no need for conflicting candidates since no conflicting classes exist in the USSR, Mr. Arutyunyan, according to Peter Grose, said:

> Our socialist democracy should ever work to a higher stage of development.
> In our country the people and the classes are all united. But this unity does not mean a complete homogeneity of all the opinions and feelings of the people, of their talents and energies, their methods of work and public activity.
> Therefore, the nomination of more than one candidate would in no way violate the unity of the voters. It would, on the other hand, increase their public activity and interest, would raise the level of responsibility of the candidates toward their electors.

While so far as I know this matter has not reached the stage of serious consideration in Party and Government circles, it is of great interest that a question of this kind, suggesting such a drastic departure from previous Party policy, should have been raised publicly by a leading Party and Government official.

How Candidates Are Nominated

THE basic official reason always given for it not being necessary to have a choice of candidates is that because there are no antagonistic classes in the Soviet Union and no clash of contending interests, it is natural that the people should arrive at a unanimous choice in their nominating meetings. At these meetings several names are frequently brought forward. They are names well known to the

community, and there is very full and free discussion of the qualifications of each person proposed. Often candidates will themselves withdraw in favor of the candidate who appears to be most popular. These nominating discussions are often quite prolonged. Very often, unanimity is achieved in the course of the discussion. If not, the decision is reached by majority vote. Sometimes other organizations or other meetings may endorse the candidate put forward by the first meeting.

If different candidates are proposed by different groups, then a meeting is called of elected representatives of all the groups and organizations concerned in the given election district. At such meetings there is sometimes unanimous agreement on a single candidate. Otherwise the single candidate is determined by majority vote.

Descriptions of these meetings given me by a variety of people have been very convincing as to the open way voters speak their minds and analyze the qualifications of prospective candidates to perform their duties and look after their constituents' interests. This democratic process probably works best in the smaller towns and villages and electoral districts where all the people know each other very well. The candidate is sometimes present and has to give an account of himself.

On the other hand, I have heard of nominating meetings in large cities where the process is more cut and dried. Fewer people may turn out to meetings; they may, through cynicism or indifference, simply accept whoever is proposed without discussion. This would probably not be true in a factory, but might happen in some government or academic institution. I have seen descriptions in both Soviet and other sources, of nominating meetings of a purely ceremonial nature where people are called together merely to accept by acclamation candidates presented to them in formal speeches with bands and banners to create a festive atmosphere, and little room for discussion.

While this ceremonial type of nominating meeting may often take place in large cities, it is by no means always like that. For example, there was the case of Mikhail Shavrin, Chairman of a district Soviet in Leningrad. In the 1964 elections, when he was again proposed for the office at a factory meeting, a number of the workers objected. Several speakers described him as a man who often displayed callousness and bureaucratic methods in his work and was unworthy of representing them. His candidacy was rejected by majority vote. (Cited in pamphlet *Political Democracy in the USSR* by G. Moiseyev and A. Ardotavsky, published by USSR Embassy, London, 1965.)

The practice of nominating candidates and the extent of discussion around them thus may be seen to vary greatly from place to place, and time to time, as is true of many other aspects of Soviet life. The trend is in the direction of more and more democratic procedures.

After the candidate is chosen and his or her acceptance secured, the candidacy must be approved and registered by the election committee set up in each district on the basis of elected representatives from all leading community organizations and groups.

Election centers are set up around which the election campaign is organized and through which propaganda and educational work on government policies and issues of special concern to the voters locally is carried on.

The candidates have no individual campaign expenses. All expenses connected with election meetings, canvassing, printing, pamphlets and whatever, are met by the government. Every candidate gets all the publicity desired, the people demanding to be very fully informed both of the past record and future intentions of all candidates. A candidate is called upon to speak frequently, at meetings where the voters have full opportunity to ask questions and present their demands. The voters are very insistent that the candidates be fully informed about what their constituents expect from them. Thus the campaigns are by no means routine affairs, and the deputies are held severely to the fulfillment of pre-election pledges.

Election day is made a festive occasion throughout the country. People congratulate each other as on a holiday. Young people especially, voting for the first time, are made to feel the importance of the act. In factories and construction projects new records in production are chalked up for the occasion. It is a time of summing up achievements, and making new plans and pledges for the future.

At the polls on election day, the voter, whether in Supreme Soviet or local elections, is handed a ballot on which the name of one can-

Fellow Deputies at the Moscow Supreme Soviet: The late Yuri Gagarin, famous cosmonaut, chatting with machine operator Clara Bekeshova from Gurevo region (center) and Merivart Kindikbaeva, collective farm field brigade worker from Kazakhstan.

didate is written for deputy to each of the one or more Soviets involved, or other office. (Elections may be for district, regional and city Soviets simultaneously.) He may simply signify his consent by putting it into the ballot box as is. He may, if he wishes, go into a curtained booth, and vote against any candidate by crossing out his name. There is no provision for write-in votes. Any candidate receiving a majority of the votes is elected. If a candidate receives less than a majority of the votes, he is not elected. In such an event new nominating meetings and new elections must be held within two weeks. (This happens most frequently in local Soviet elections.)

The voter is further protected by the right to recall any deputy not satisfying his constituents. The procedure in case of demand for recall is the convening of special electors' meetings by the *Ispolkom* (executive committee) of the appropriate Soviet or the Presidium of the Supreme Soviet. The decision to recall requires a majority vote, taken by show of hands. A new election is then conducted to replace the deputy or other office-holder recalled.

The Right of Recall

NIKOLAY PODGORNY, President of the Presidium of the Supreme Soviet, reported at the 23rd Congress of the CPSU in June, 1966 (see *Soviet Life*, July, 1966) that the Soviet people were making more demands on their deputies than ever before. He said that during the preceding year (1965-1966) more than 350 deputies had been recalled at all levels. While 350 may not seem a very large number out of a total of two million deputies, it is the largest number yet reported, and shows that this guarantee of the people's rights is real and active.

There have also been a number of cases when People's Judges have been recalled by their electors. One such case was reported in *Soviet Weekly* (June 25, 1966).

It happened in the village of Verkhny Kurash, in the Bashkir Autonomous Republic. The district People's Judge, Minigaley Sharafutdinov, refused to bring proceedings against an assistant in the cooperative store, who had been found to have embezzled the store's funds by associates who had the goods on him. Indignant cooperative members demanded that the judge attend a meeting and explain his action. Since he had acted in a similar arrogant manner in the past, failing to enter other cases for trial within the time prescribed by law, refusing in general to report on his work to the electors as required and seldom being available to callers, the question of his recall was raised before the District Soviet.

The District Soviet's Standing Commission on questions of law and order investigated and found the complaints against the judge justified. Some members of the commission urged that the judge simply be reprimanded, but the majority advised a recall. Meetings were then called in the villages that made up the district. Sharafutdinov rushed around mobilizing people to defend him, and some indeed did. There were hot discussions at all the meetings. The judge admitted his mistakes and asked for another chance. The consensus of opinion, however, was that Sharafutdinov had not justified the confidence that had been placed in him by the electors. He had shown himself unfit to be a judge, "had a rude attitude toward people" and refused even to listen to their wishes. The final result was that 13,932 of the district's 17,628 electors voted for his recall, way over the majority required for such action.

The Supreme Soviet

IN THE elections of June 12, 1966 to the Seventh USSR Supreme Soviet, all 1,517 candidates were elected—767 deputies to the Soviet of the Union, 750 to the Soviet of Nationalities. Of the country's 144 million registered voters, 99.94 per cent voted. The candidates for deputy to the Soviet of the Union received the votes of 99.76 per cent of the voters, with 345,643 ballots marked against the candidate listed. The candidates to the Soviet of Nationalities were supported by 99.80 per cent of the voters, 289,298 voting against. No candidates failed to receive a majority of the votes.

The composition of the Congress shows how close the deputies are to the interests of the people. Of the 1,517 deputies, 698 are workers and collective farmers; over 300 engineers; 200 agronomists and other agricultural experts. The remaining 300 are from the various arts and professions and people who work in government, economic, Party, trade union or Komsomol (Communist Youth League) organizations. The overwhelming majority are members of trade unions who thus play a direct part in making the laws affecting labor, just as the large number of collective farmers guarantee that their special interests are represented. Workers and collective farmers comprise 45.3 per cent of the Soviet of Nationalities, 46.7 per cent of the Soviet of the Union.

Of the deputies elected to the Seventh Supreme Soviet, 425 (28 per cent), were women. (In the U.S. Congress, two out of 100 Senators are women, and nine out of 435 members of the House of Representatives, or 2 per cent of the total in both cases.) Some 200 of the deputies were under 30 years of age.

About two-thirds of the deputies were elected for the first time, in line with the decision of the 22nd Party Congress that fresh blood be constantly infused into all government and party bodies.

Of the 1,517 deputies, 1,141 were Party members and candidates, the proportion of non-Party members (24 per cent) being about equal in both houses. The proportion of non-Party members in the local Soviets is much higher than in the Supreme Soviet, sometimes reaching fifty per cent. There is a strong effort to bring forward as many non-Party people as possible as deputies, forming what is designated as the "Bloc of Communists and non-Party people."

In the Soviet of Nationalities, 57 different nationalities and peoples are represented; in the Soviet of the Union, 37.

A unique feature of the Soviet Parliament is that no one is paid to be a member of Congress. All the MPs pursue their regular jobs or professions. Among the deputies you will find every kind of person in the Soviet Union. Top government leaders are deputies, and along with them miners and textile workers, tractor drivers and beet growers, collective farm chairmen, leading scientists, teachers and doctors, poets and cosmonauts, top academicians and herdsmen from the Far North, and no doubt, cooks, every one of whom Lenin once said "must learn to run the government."

Among the deputies to the Supreme Soviet of the RSFSR, largest of the Union Republics, is L. A. Sysoyeva, a twenty-five year old milkmaid from the Zvenigorod State Farm in Moscow Province. In a speech at the 23rd CPSU Congress, she made some very useful and concrete suggestions on the organization of milkmaids' labor, in the course of a discussion of agriculture. She also told what it meant to her to be a deputy to the Supreme Soviet of her republic. Here (translated from *Pravda,* April 5, 1966) are some of the remarks she made:

> A worker's sense of pride—that is a great feeling! Two years ago I visited America with our youth delegation. . . . In order to show us what kind of freedom they have in the U.S.A., they arranged a meeting for us with American Senators. There was a lot of talk about democracy, they praised their American system, but then something misfired. They asked me who I was. I answered that I was a deputy to the Supreme Soviet of the RSFSR, and a milkmaid by occupation.
>
> I remember as clearly as if it were today how long their faces grew. Of course that was understandable. There are no dairymaids in their Congress, democracy doesn't permit it. Then some of our hosts decided to test me out. In the city of Syracuse one of them, Mr. Lee, asked me to show him my hands. . . . "Very well, Mr. Lee," I said, "please have a look—here they are. ordinary workers' hands."
>
> But that wasn't enough either. And when we were guests of an American farmer, Mr. Lescher, they asked me again: "Now show us how you milk the cows in Russia." So I did the evening milking for him. And Mr. Lescher had to acknowledge that in the Soviet Union Members of Parliament, too, know how to milk cows. . . .

Only a very small proportion of the deputies needed for full time work on the Presidium, which acts between sessions, are paid workers of the Soviet. In general, deputies are paid only expenses of travel and housing connected with attending Soviet sessions.

Deputies are required to set aside a certain number of days each month in which to see their constituents and hear their complaints and requirements. The hours and place of reception must be publicized so that the people know when and where to go. It is required that any factory, enterprise or other place of work make the necessary arrangements for the deputies' release from work for the required number of hours. Extension of periods of release for specialized work has been under consideration recently, and no doubt something will be done about this.

How Soviet Laws Are Made

WHENEVER an important piece of legislation is envisaged, as already noted, a draft is prepared by an appropriate commission of the Supreme Soviet on the basis of proposals received from a variety of sources. This draft is then published in the press and spread far and wide and meetings are held everywhere from the big cities to the smallest localities and collective farms, with millions of people taking part. The drafting commission takes into consideration the suggestions and amendments sent in as a result of these nationwide discussions, in drawing up the new draft for presentation. Further amendments are made at the Supreme Soviet session, although these are usually not extensive since by this time the opinions of the people are pretty well reflected. Recent years have seen somewhat more critical discussions at the Supreme Soviet sessions than was previously the case. Public organizations such as trade unions, youth groups, women's councils and others may initiate legislation.

Through these nationwide discussions on new legislation or changes in existing legislation the government keeps in very close contact with the wishes of the people and the people as a whole have a very real part in the making of the laws. Such discussions took place on the reorganization of the Machine and Tractor Stations, when new civil and criminal codes were drawn up, when the educational reform introduced by Khrushchev was under discussion and when it was later modified, on the new pension law, on draft five-year plans. The draft of the 1959-65 seven-year plan, for example, was discussed at nearly a million meetings of over 70 million people. Many modifications and changes are introduced as a result of these discussions. Measures are being considered to incorporate criticism and proposals advanced during discussions even more fully. The submission of All-Union bills for prior consideration by local Soviets is being discussed.

These public discussions amount almost to national plebiscites in scope and opportunities for the expression of public opinion. Naturally no one is naive enough to suppose that there can be no manipulation of even such widespread discussions. There are many ways in which the official viewpoint may be presented to influence its acceptance. But there is no doubt in my mind that the official viewpoint is in itself very largely determined by the needs and wishes of the people, that the use of coercion in imposing it has disappeared and that more and more in recent years people are speaking out frankly and fearlessly against whatever they feel to be mistakes or abuses of power and for what they consider right.

The widespread use of letters to the press for the redress of grievances or initiation of new measures must also be mentioned. All newspapers have special departments for this and hundreds of thousands of citizens express themselves in this form. Whether or not the letters are published, it is a hard and fast rule that any specific complaint be looked into and taken care of where justified, and that general complaints or suggestions be turned over to appropriate government or other organs to be taken into consideration.

EACH of the fifteen Union Republics has its own one-chamber Supreme Soviet, with its Presidium, Council of Ministers and Supreme Court. Each has its own Constitution and makes its own laws on internal matters, which must, however, be in accord with the USSR Constitution. In the Council of Ministers of the USSR there are certain all-Union ministries dealing with the affairs of the country as a whole. Others exist both for the USSR and for the separate republics, while still others dealing with specifically local affairs, exist only in the Union Republics. Union republics which contain autonomous republics and autonomous regions include representatives of these republics and regions as vice presidents of their Supreme Soviet presidiums. The highest organs of power in the autonomous republics are similar in principle to those in the union republics.

At the base of the pyramid whose apex is the Supreme Soviet we have in the countryside the village Soviet, above that the district Soviet, covering a whole group of villages, and above that the regional or territorial Soviet. The large cities are divided up into districts which each have their own Soviets as well as being covered by the City Soviet as a whole. And above the City Soviet is the regional or territorial Soviet that covers both city and countryside.

During the Khrushchev period, after his policy of dividing the Party at all lower levels into industrial sections and agricultural sections went into effect, the Soviets often followed suit. While this worked out all right in districts that were wholly industrial or wholly agricultural, in most areas of the country there is to one extent or another an admixture of both, and in these places the division led to incredible confusion, with duplication of effort in some cases and neglect of important functions in others. From the end of 1962 to the end of 1964 there were separate industrial and rural Soviets in two-thirds of the regions of the USSR.

When I was in the Soviet Union in 1964 the division was still in force, and the people's dissatisfaction with it was very apparent.

Within a month after Khrushchev's replacement, the division was ended and the traditional unity of both Party and State administrative structures was restored at all levels.

17

Chapter 2

THE LOCAL SOVIETS

THE local Soviets are the organs of government closest to the people, concerned with everything that touches their daily lives. Through them the people are being increasingly drawn into the work of self-government on a volunteer basis. Today, almost one out of every ten of the entire population or about one out of five of the adult population of the Soviet Union does such volunteer work.

Before describing the operation of the local Soviets today, it is important to look back and see how V. I. Lenin envisaged their development in the very early days of the Revolution. In an article in *Izvestia* on April 28, 1918, "The Immediate Tasks of the Soviet Government," Lenin wrote:

> We must work tirelessly to develop the organization of the Soviets and the Soviet Government. There is a petty bourgeois tendency to transform the members of the Soviets into "Members of Parliament," or into bureaucrats. This must be combatted by drawing *all* the members of the Soviets into the practical work of administration. In many places the departments of the Soviets are gradually becoming merged with the Commissiariats. Our aim is to draw the *whole of the poor* into the practical work of administration, and every step that is taken in this direction—the more varied they are, the better—should be carefully ·registered, studied, systematized, tested by wide experience and passed into law. Our aim is to insure that *every* toiler, after having finished his eight hours "lesson" in productive labor, shall perform state duties *gratis*: the transition to this is a particularly difficult one, but this transition alone can guarantee the final consolidation of socialism.
>
> Naturally, the novelty and difficulty of the change gives rise to an abundance of steps taken, as it were gropingly, to an abundance of mistakes and vacillations—without this rapid progress is impossible. . . .
>
> It is not sufficient to be a revolutionary and an adherent of socialism, or a communist in general. One must be able at each particular moment to find that special link in the chain which one must grasp with all one's might in order to hold the whole chain, and to make lasting preparations for the transition to the next link; the order of the links, their form, the manner in which they are linked together, their difference from each other in the historical chain of events, are not as simple and not as senseless as those in an ordinary chain made by a smith.
>
> The fight against the bureaucratic distortion of the Soviet organization is made secure by the firmness of the connection between the Soviets

and the "people," meaning by that the toilers and exploited, and by the flexibility and elasticity of this connection. Even in the most democratic capitalist republic in the world, the poor never regard the bourgeois parliament as "their own" institution. But the Soviets are "their own" and not alien institutions to the masses of workers and peasants.

It is precisely the closeness of the Soviets to the "people," to the toilers, that creates the special forms of recall and control from below which must be most zealously developed now. For example, the Councils of People's Education, as periodical conferences of Soviet electors and their delegates called to discuss and control the activities of the Soviet authorities in a given field, are deserving of full sympathy and support. Nothing would be sillier than to transform the Soviets into something congealed and self-contained. The more resolutely we now have to stand for a ruthlessly firm government, for the dictatorship of individual persons, *in definite processes of work,* in definite aspects of *purely executive* functions, the more varied must be the forms and methods of control from below in order to counteract every shadow of possibility of distorting the Soviet power, in order repeatedly and tirelessly to weed out bureaucracy.

While this conception of the role of the Soviets has never been abandoned, it is actually only in recent years that it has begun to be fully realized in practice.

In the Early Days

DURING the lifetime of Lenin, and even in the first years after his death, the Soviets played an extremely important role as local organs of government. They had a lot of responsibility in government administration not only at the local level, but in considering questions of national and republic significance. In many cases it was the Soviets which took over the actual direction of industrial enterprises, both in the period of restoration of the limited and badly crippled industry inherited from the old regime, and at the beginning of the industrialization program.

In the very early days when the new society was still in its infancy, the Soviets functioned under great difficulties. There was a great lack of manpower. Throughout all the disasters of the period of the world war, civil war, intervention, famine, typhus and other epidemics, the ranks of the best and most politically conscious people were decimated. The ranks of the Communists, trained in a leadership role, and always first to give examples to others and to sacrifice themselves, suffered most of all. There were far too few people available for the massive job, only tardily started, of pushing and pulling the great backward land they inherited from the Nineteenth into the Twentieth Century and at the same time establishing a social structure never known on earth before.

In the villages I knew in the early twenties, when I was doing famine relief work with the American Friends Service Committee (Quakers), most of the adults were still illiterate. There were very few people available for positions of leadership in the party and government. Elections under these conditions were still almost meaningless, and whoever was available somehow got the administrative posts. In these jobs one would find remarkable, devoted personalities, efficient and concerned only with serving the people. But in numerous cases the "chinovnik" type—bureaucratic, stupid, self-seeking creatures right out of Gogol's *Inspector General*—had managed to get hold of whatever official posts were open. They were accepted because they were literate, if nothing else, even though barely so, and accustomed to drawing up "AKTS." This meant writing out a decision or instructions in stilted, formal language, affixing official signatures in purple ink with huge flourishes, and stamping the resulting "dokument" with a huge seal. Whether you wanted some nails or a house to live in in those early days, nothing would come of it without an "AKT." And very often that was all that did come of it!

Among these *chinovnik* types there were just plain knaves or thieves who simply wanted to use their official positions, and did, to get for themselves whatever material things were available when there was only enough for a very few. There were others who were merely opportunists, ready to serve whatever regime was in power, who managed to get into the ranks of the Communist Party.

It must not be forgotten that there were also counter-revolutionary elements who managed to get hold of official posts, with the deliberate purpose of restoring the old regime, wrecking the new one from within before it could even get started (and afterwards as well), sabotaging the world's first socialist state by messing things up in whatever way possible to demonstrate that socialism just couldn't work.

And there were plenty of others, good honest people, who wanted to do things right but just didn't know how, who also messed things up.

Everything had to be done at once—the repairing of the vast damage, the "liquidation of illiteracy," the building up of a modern, industrialized country from the beginning, not only with no help from the outside, but with obstacles and hostile plots attempting to prevent them at every step.

No people in history had ever faced such a gigantic job against such unimaginable odds. There were not enough trained people to go around. The best of them were needed on the big industrialization projects, in the new factories, the new state farms, the new electric power plants, the new railroads. Neither was there enough proper leadership to man the official positions in the Soviets, nor enough people available to spread out their functions on a volunteer basis.

Thus, in those early days, the members of our relief group came into contact with many fine people working in the Soviets and with many quite the opposite. I can remember that at one point in Sorochinskoye the whole Mutual Aid Committee attached to the

Soviet, which helped in the allocation and distribution of food rations, was arrested and tried for having presented to the Quakers a list of "dead souls" for whom rations were provided, which instead this little gang of thieves distributed among themselves. They were replaced by an honest and reliable group.

I can remember that in all those early years, the word *ispolkom* —that is, the executive committee of the village or town or district or city Soviet—came to be synonymous with something bumbling, bureaucratic, standing in the way of the people and their needs rather than helping them out.

Ispolkom offices were thronged with people from morning until night. Even to get to see the officials seemed an almost hopeless task. It meant waiting around for endless hours or maybe days before getting anyone's attention, then being sent to another department and to another, and very likely going away empty-handed in the end. With no materials available and skilled workmen needed in the factories, how was it possible to do major repairs on apartment buildings? With housing falling into ruin, with thousands of people pouring into the towns from the countryside, with families crowded in together in whatever decent apartments there were, there were few whose needs could be satisfied and the majority went away grumbling. It was a thankless task indeed to be a member of a Soviet in those days.

As things grew better materially the Soviets began to function better and more democratically. Yet with the forced tempo of industrialization and collectivization under the five-year plans, problems of goods and clothing and housing still unsolved, the ordinary business of life was too difficult for people to spend much time on the very important and desirable process of learning the art of self-government.

As the new modern industrialized society began to rise, as education became universal, the Soviets and their democratic functioning were supposed to rise with it. They were given new and extended functions under the new Constitution of 1936, which were in fact left unrealized.

Through all this period the Soviet people were performing miracles of growth and construction, a strong basis was being laid for the future flowering of a socialist society.

Distortions in the Stalin Era

SIDE by side with this healthy growth, another process was taking place, a process that had no place in a normal socialist society. This was the outgrowth of Stalin's theory that the class struggle sharpened with the consolidation of socialism, which contradicted Lenin's that it would lessen. And this was exacerbated by Stalin's paranoia which meant building himself up to a pinnacle of omnipotence, along with an ever-growing suspicion of anyone who might disagree even a hairsbreadth with him. This led to the designation of thousands upon thousands of innocent people as "enemies of the people" who had to be suppressed or destroyed. Their persecution required a vast police apparatus which grew up as a second power beside the power of the people's state and stunted and distorted the growth of the latter.

The resultant excessive centralization of government administration and growth of bureaucracy led to a sharp decline in the role of the Soviets during this period. The local Soviets no longer had any real responsibility for local affairs. Everything had to be checked with higher authorities and central agencies. Local initiative was paralyzed. This led to "stereotyped and paper-pushing modes of operation" of Soviets at all levels.*

An article in *Kommunist*, No. 2, for 1962, in preparation for the March 1962 elections to the Supreme Soviet, pointed out that the flagrant offenses against Soviet law during the period of the Stalin cult also encroached on the democratic rights of the Union Republics within the USSR and restricted the work of democratic institutions at all levels. "Restrictions of Soviet democracy that were inevitable in the early days of the Revolution at the time of the struggle against the class enemy," the article said, "were elevated by Stalin to a regular practice." This led to hypertrophy of the executive apparatus of government, to the belittling of the role of the Soviets as representative mass organizations, and to depreciating Lenin's thesis of the Soviets as schools of government.

Thus, the article charged, the Stalin cult crippled the growth of socialist democracy, hindered the progress of the Soviet system, and retarded the development of the initiative of the masses. "The most important task today," said *Kommunist*, "is to promote the role of the Soviets as organs of the absolute rule of the people in all spheres of social life . . . as the most representative organization of the working people, expressing their will."

Particularly criticized in the article was the tendency during the Stalin period for Party organizations to supplant the Soviets. The Party, the article pointed out, should give assistance and guidance but should never assume the functions of government or mass organizations. This point has been emphasized in many articles in leading Soviet journals in recent years.

While the millions of the Soviet people went about their work and accomplished wonders of Socialist construction, there was at the same time this ugly repressive power raising obstacles to their work, stifling their initiative, hampering their progress. The tragedy was

* See article "Increasing the Role of the Soviets: An Immediate Task," by V. Chkhikvadze, I. Pavlov and I. Azovkin, *Sovety Deputatov Trudiashchikhsia*, 1965, No. 8. Translation published in *Soviet Sociology*, International Arts and Sciences Press, Spring 1966, Vol IV, No. 4.

that Stalin did not trust the people, even though he could utter such beautiful phrases as "Only the people are immortal."

None of the methods used by Stalin can be condoned. Yet there are two points that must never be forgotten.

One is that the essence of socialism always remained. The phrase "only the people are immortal," even while Stalin himself and many around him were betraying it, was engraved in the hearts of the people. Social ownership of the means of production, the foundation stone of the socialist state, remained secure.

The other is the guilt of the outside world. While the plots against the Soviet state and against Stalin himself, for which so many died needlessly, were products of a mind growing increasingly sick and continuously inflamed by sycophants and evil people around him, there were from the beginning numerous very real plots in the capitalist world, using whatever allies they could find within, for the destruction of the world's first socialist state. Without the real plots against the socialist state, the outright military efforts to destroy it, the hostility of the whole capitalist world expressed both overtly and covertly, there would have been no soil to nourish Stalin's suspicions.

During World War II and After

AND even despite all this, the Soviet state grew and flourished and there was beginning to be a more solid material base and a steady advance of education and flowering of culture. As the fascist menace rose, the USSR made mighty efforts to establish collective security. But then came Munich and World War II and the invasion by Hitler.

In those years the Soviet people saw vast areas laid waste and twenty million of their people perish and a third of the industry built over the years with sweat and tears and blood wiped out. And in those years the Soviets like every other part of Soviet society could have no other concern than doing their part to support the war effort, and the extension of democracy could take no other form than the extension of the democracy of common sacrifice and common effort.

After victory came the years of reconstruction and new beginnings and new growth and the cold war outside to try to hold them back, and inside an intensification of Stalin's suspicions and new repressions and terrors and wild happenings like the incredible doctors' plot, events that hampered and slowed up Soviet progress but could never succeed in completely damming the great forward surge of the people.

But it was only the Twentieth Congress of the CPSU, with the revelations about Stalin's excesses, exposing the dark secrets of the past, ending the police state apparatus, opening up the prison camps, that freed the people's creative initiative again.

116300

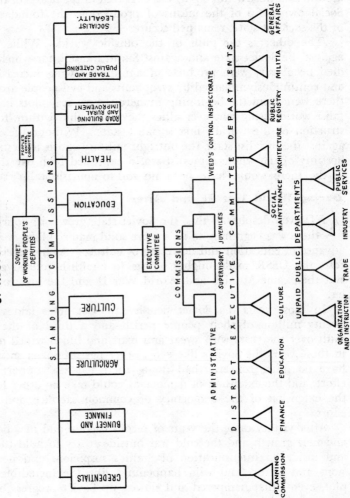

STRUCTURAL SET-UP
OF SALSK DISTRICT SOVIET OF WORKING PEOPLE'S DEPUTIES
OF ROSTOV REGION

SOVIET OF WORKING PEOPLE'S DEPUTIES

PEOPLE'S CONTROL COMMITTEE

STANDING COMMISSIONS

CREDENTIALS

BUDGET AND FINANCE

AGRICULTURE

CULTURE

EDUCATION

HEALTH

ROAD BUILDING AND RURAL IMPROVEMENT

TRADE AND PUBLIC CATERING

SOCIALIST LEGALITY

EXECUTIVE COMMITTEE

COMMISSIONS

SUPERVISORY

JUVENILES

WEED'S CONTROL INSPECTORATE

ADMINISTRATIVE

DISTRICT EXECUTIVE COMMITTEE DEPARTMENTS

PLANNING COMMISSION

FINANCE

EDUCATION

CULTURE

SOCIAL MAINTENANCE

ARCHITECTURE

PUBLIC REGISTRY

MILITIA

GENERAL AFFAIRS

UNPAID PUBLIC DEPARTMENTS

ORGANIZATION AND INSTRUCTION

TRADE

INDUSTRY

PUBLIC SERVICES

On the basis of directives of the Twentieth Congress regarding the need to revivify the Soviets, the CPSU Central Committee passed a resolution in January, 1957, "On Improving the Functioning of the Soviets of Working People's Deputies and Strengthening Their Ties With the Masses." This resolution envisaged greater responsibility of the local Soviets in the work of industry, agriculture, housing, schools, hospitals and in fact all community enterprises serving the population. It stressed that Party committees must not interfere in the functions of Government organs. Party organizations were directed to put an end to all petty tutelage and unnecessary interference in the work of the Soviets and insure the development of their initiative and independence. The 22nd Party Congress and the new Party program outlined even broader activities for local government, and especially wider participation of the people in the work of the Soviets and in people's self-government. The 23rd Congress in 1966 confirmed these measures and proposed to carry them further.

Meantime, a whole series of Government decrees outlined concrete implementation of these measures, carried them still further and made them the law of the land.

Volunteer Work in Soviets

THE main form of insuring the active participation of all citizens in the running of the government naturally had to be through the local Soviets in both city and countryside. This meant first placing greater responsibilities on the deputies themselves, requiring their active participation in all phases of the work of the Soviets, and insuring their ever greater contact with the people in their districts and their problems. They must hold regular office hours, report regularly to their constituents. Often Soviet sessions are held in factories and other institutions, taking the Soviet directly to the people. But even more important, and based on the activity of the deputies themselves, was the drawing of vast masses of the people into volunteer work with the Soviets, giving them an active part in solving the problems of their own day-to-day lives.

The extent to which this has been accomplished in the last few years may be seen from the fact that there are at present in the Soviet Union some 47,000 Soviets at all levels, with 2,000,000 elected deputies. And in addition to these, there are 23,000,000 active volunteer workers who are an integral part of the Soviets, and this number grows all the time.

The way in which this work is organized is this. After the deputies to the Soviet are elected, a general meeting of the Soviet elects an *Ispolkom* (Executive Committee) of from 11 to 15 members. The *Ispolkom* elects its officers—Chairman, Deputy Chairman and Secretary—these probably being the only full-time, paid workers from among the *Ispolkom* members. The *Ispolkom* is responsible for the setting up and manning of the regular departments of the Soviet. These are similar to the Departments that would be found in any village, town or city council in our country, although no doubt more comprehensive, covering every phase of Soviet life.

They include departments of budget and finance, housing, communal services, transportation, education, health, culture, welfare, industry and or agriculture, trade and so on, with others added according to any special features or needs of the locality.

These departments are headed by an elected member of the Soviet, with the appropriate qualifications, and manned by qualified staff people, non-members of the Soviet, usually paid workers. Thus the housing department is usually headed by an architect or construction engineer, the education department by someone with teaching experience, the health department by a doctor and so on.

Volunteers are to some extent drawn into the work of the departments of the Soviets. But the main avenue through which the people's participation in the Soviets is effected is through the standing commissions which supplement the work of the regular Soviet departments. Heads of these standing commissions are elected from among the deputies at a full meeting of the Soviet immediately following elections. Deputies are not paid for heading the standing commissions. It is part of their regular work as deputies. None of the members of the standing commissions are paid. Qualified volunteers are drawn in to do the work. They cover fields corresponding in the main to the Departments of the *Ispolkom* and coordinate their work with them.

In order to keep these standing commissions separate from the *Ispolkom* and its departments, and to prevent the *Ispolkom* members from exerting too strong an influence on them, the regulations in some of the constituent republics provide that none of the members of the *Ispolkom* can serve on the standing commissions. Other republics provide that members of the *Ispolkom* may not be elected chairman, deputy chairman or secretary of the commissions. Still others provide that deputies who are the heads of Departments of the *Ispolkom* may not be elected to official positions in the standing commissions. The number of members of the commissions varies according to local conditions and needs, usually being from five to twenty, while the voluntary "actives" of the commissions are not limited in number ,and may vary from time to time as special projects require.

The chairman and members of the standing commissions are usually elected at a session of the Soviet. The deputy chairman, if there is to be one, and the secretary are elected at the first meeting of the standing commission. In some republics, all the officers are elected at a meeting of the full Soviet; in others all the officers are elected by the standing commission itself.

The standing commissions consider all questions that may come up

26

in the Soviet itself, as well as other questions they may raise them-selves, or that are raised by the people among whom they work. Pre-viously, the standing commissions had the right only to *recommend action.* Since April 1962, their recommendations have become *ob-ligatory,* in some, though not yet all, of the Soviets.

The standing commissions have the responsibility of checking on the fulfillment of all party and government decisions, on the func-tioning of all enterprises and municipal services under the supervision of the Soviet, and also of checking on the work of the departments of the *Ispolkom.* They may raise the question of changing the personnel of the departments if they do not do their work properly. They have the right to call before them for questioning the head of any enterprise or institution.

The standing commissions draw into their work specialists in vari-ous fields who are employed in some institution but are prepared to volunteer a certain amount of their time for work with the Soviet. They enlist housewives who are willing to give part of their time regularly, as well as workers and collective farmers. They especially attract a great many pensioners who are glad of an opportunity to pursue their professions after retirement.

All affairs of the standing commissions are decided by a majority vote of those present (which must usually be more than half of the membership, although the requirement is two-thirds in some Repub-lics) .

The official regulations require regular reports by the standing commissions to the Soviet, usually quarterly. They sometimes meet monthly, sometimes less often. Government regulations caution against too frequent meetings as detrimental to active, creative work and emphasize that the main concern of the standing commissions must be systematic, organizational activities with the masses of the people at their places of work and their homes.

There is considerable variation in the effectiveness of the work of these standing commissions between one place and another.

In the country as a whole, the operation of the standing commis-sions has led to a very sharp decrease in the number of paid Soviet of-ficials and civil servants generally. There have been instances where the standing committees have been able to replace completely the regular departments of the *Ispolkom,* and to do away entirely with paid personnel in certain fields, except for purely technical help.

Chapter 3

CITY SOVIETS IN IRKUTSK AND KIEV

DURING a visit to the Soviet Union in 1961, I found a big nation-wide effort already under way to enhance both the role of the Soviets and the role of the people in them. But the work of the volunteers, of which much is now being made, was still of a rather limited nature, and involved mainly the drawing in of the whole population in the planting of trees and shrubbery, clean-up and beautification campaigns in the cities and similar matters.

The Irkutsk City Soviet

IN JUNE, 1961, Siberia's early springtime, I was sitting in the office of Mayor Ivanov of Irkutsk. He had brought together several other city officials to answer my questions.

I noticed on this trip that officials I met, whether city, party, industrial or whatever, were a new type of people. In earlier years, while there were many fine and able people in such jobs, there was still an indefinable quality of the former bureaucratic officialdom about many of them. A certain traditional aura still clung to every office per se, irrespective of the person who might be holding it. I don't doubt that that type is still to be found. But in my two trips of the sixties, officials I met were of a quite different caliber. They were efficient, energetic, knowledgeable about all the practical aspects of their work, and very close to the people and the life around them.

Mayor Ivanov of Irkutsk had the outgoing, effervescent quality I found in most East Siberians. He was silvery-haired though still very young looking, with bright, laughing blue eyes. A true patriot of his city, as I found all Soviet mayors to be, he spent quite a lot of time singing the praises of Irkutsk and Siberia before getting down to my questions.

"I was born in Kharkov," he told me, "and came here in 1939. Of course I was at the front during all the war years—but Siberia had gotten under my skin and I came right back here when the war was over. Now I am completely acclimatized.

"I like the life here. It is stormy, impetuous, straining forward like a race horse—this is the quality of East Siberia and its people. The people of Irkutsk have tremendous enthusiasm for their city."

Irkutsk, with a population at the time of 381,000 people, had a City Soviet to which 449 deputies had been elected the preceding

March, and also four District Soviets, with 900 newly elected deputies altogether.

Getting down to the actual functioning of the Soviets, there were the usual regular departments—health, education, housing, industrial, cultural, and others—with the corresponding standing commissions headed by deputies elected at Soviet sessions and made up entirely of volunteers (although large-scale volunteer work was not yet well developed). Ivanov stressed the close ties of the Soviet officials and deputies with the people of the city.

"About once a month," Ivanov said, "every member of our *Ispolkom* (Executive Committee) reports at some factory or enterprise. For example, in May I made a report to the workers of the Kuibyshev machine-building plant. On June 1st, I reported to the workers of the Angara Hydroelectric Station. We also try to get as many rank and file people from the city as possible to attend our regular Soviet sessions. The people criticize us freely, we try to meet their requests and suggestions for improvement. We have big public meetings whenever new legislation is discussed. Before the new decree on the school reform was passed, we had public discussions to which we invited teachers and school directors; hundreds of people took part."

Ivanov explained that most of the work of volunteers was carried on through the District Soviets rather than the main City Soviet. The inhabitants of each district are organized into street and apartment house committees and take part in the work of the Soviet through these committees.

Formerly the trade departments of the District Soviets, with a paid staff, had the responsibility of looking after the work of the stores and trade organizations and keeping it up to scratch. But after sending a delegation to Sverdlovsk to study their methods, volunteers were now investigating the conditions in the stores, checking up on early supply and distribution and making recommendations to the proper authorities.

Beautification of the city was at that time one of the main volunteer projects.

"This year," Ivanov told me, "in honor of our city's 300th anniversary, our people decided to plant trees and flowers on a wider scale than ever. Look around the city and you will see the results! The people do this in their spare time. Last year 130,000 trees were planted. About 400,000 man hours were given, one for each member of our population! This year the people themselves have decided to do about twice as much.

"Last year, five million flowering plants were planted in the city. This year millions more. Mainly we are planting cultivated flowers. But we need more perennials. We've had a big argument raging about why we can't bring in the wild flowers that grow in such abundance in the taiga. Our oldtime specialists insist they can't be adapted to city conditions. But now we are experimenting with this and maybe a way can be found."

And what is the biggest problem of all in Irkutsk?

"Housing, housing and again housing! With so many new people streaming out to Siberia, that's the main problem we must solve. We keep building faster and faster, but it's never enough. Last year we built 120,000 square meters of new housing, this year it will be 150,000 and by 1965-66 we expect to be building a million square meters annually. We're using more and more prefabricated concrete panels for building. We used to import them from other parts of the country. Now we are building our own ferro-concrete plant.

"Previously our Soviet was in charge of only part of the housing construction. Now it is all in our hands. We raise some of the money for it out of our own resources, some is allocated by the RSFSR. We are building many new eight- to ten-story apartment houses; our plan is to end crowding, to have only one family to an apartment. With our great new hydroelectric stations we have all the electricity we need. All this new housing has modern plumbing and we are beginning to install electricity in the kitchens instead of gas.

"The government also provides loans for people who want to build individual homes. We try to show them how much better it is to have all the conveniences an apartment house has to offer, but many of them prefer individual houses, so let them go ahead. We have great difficulty persuading some people to move out of tumbledown old houses hardly fit for habitation: they like to have their own gardens and flowers."

There was also a big program under way for the building of new schools, kindergartens, day nurseries, additions to the polytechnical institute, new hospitals and a new hotel, a new public bath, a new cinema theater. They were adding seventeen kilometers to the single line of tramway that rambled through the length of the city, and were planning to add to the three auto bus lines already operating.

Ivanov spoke with special warmth of the work of the women. He said that one of the sad aftermaths of the war was the great excess of women over men: in Irkutsk there were some 28,000 more women than men. Now, with all the new births, the composition of the population was beginning to be equalized again.

A Talk with the Deputy Mayor of Kiev

ON MY 1964 visit, I found great changes. There had been a very big growth of the volunteer activity of the people in the Soviets in the three intervening years.

Arriving in the beautiful city of Kiev on a Saturday, in late October, my hospitable friends of the Ukrainian Society for Friendship and Cultural Relations with Foreign Countries arranged a visit for me with the deputy mayor, Boris Feodorovich Yermolovich. His working day was already over, but he courteously agreed to stay on in his office for my benefit.

He was a worker type with a rough but kind face, dressed more casually than the usual city official. His office was small and simply appointed. He sat at a small desk, with a small table at right angles to it, where I sat with Asya, my interpreter. Lacking was the huge official desk and the long table jutting out from it characteristic of the offices of most city officials, even though this was in the Ukraine's capital city, with a population of 1,300,000. I was rather glad that my interview was with the deputy mayor rather than the mayor. While all Soviet officials are hard working people, I had the impression from other interviews that the mayor himself (or herself—there are plenty of women mayors) was often more of a ceremonial figure while the deputy was closer to the everyday details of city administration.

Yermolovich asked me what I wanted to know. I told him I would like to hear from him on two things: one, the main changes that had taken place in Kiev since my last visit in 1961 and two, what was being done on the question of extending democracy through the participation of the people in the work of the Soviet.

"On your first question, in these three years there have been many changes here. We have built 2.5 million square meters of housing in that period. We have built many new schools and hospitals and a whole new section of the subway. In general our advances have been entirely along lines connected with improving the living conditions of our people.

"As to your second point on the people's participation in government, we have numerous standing commissions attached to the Soviet through which many people work voluntarily on all sorts of questions relating to the government of the city and their own needs.

"Any more questions?"

This was about the tersest answer I had ever received in all my years of asking questions in the Soviet Union. I was flabbergasted. But the interview came at the end of a long trip which had exhausted me and my sweet interpreter Asya. And no doubt Yermolovich had had a surfeit of visitors and would have liked to dispose of the interview quickly. Tempted as I was to let it go at that, I had to make one more try, so I said:

"I would like to have further details in relation to my second question about the extension of democracy through the Soviets."

He looked at me somewhat sharply, trying to size me up. Then, apparently satisfied that my question was serious, and not just idle tourist curiosity, his expression mellowed and he opened his desk drawer and took out a little book. "It's all here," he said. "I'll tell you everything you want to know." For two hours or more he held forth, describing the functions of all the standing commissions of the

City Soviet according to the regulations and adding examples of how they worked out in practice. His careful, patient detail may be judged by what follows, which is only about one-tenth of the notes I took down!

There are nine districts in the city of Kiev. The City Soviet has fourteen standing commissions, in addition to its fourteen regular departments.* The District Soviets in general have standing commissions corresponding to those of the City Soviet, according to the needs and characteristics of each district. Not all the districts need all the full standing commissions, for in some cases the City Soviet commission looks after the needs of the city as a whole. There are in all 36 standing commissions attached to the District Soviets, each with 19 or 20 members. The deputies who are commission heads and members are elected to these positions at sessions of the City Soviet. The deputies, themselves unpaid, draw in an unlimited number of volunteers according to the needs and the number of people who are interested. Volunteers who are regularly employed elsewhere give time to the Soviet after working hours. Some, like pensioners, often give full time. Many housewives give part time.

Up to 1962, these commissions had only the right to give advice and make recommendations. Now their rights have been greatly extended and their decisions are obligatory for the *Ispolkom*.

Commissions on Finance, Industry, Housing, Building

THE Commission on Budget and Finance deals with the distribution of the city budget of 1,758,000,000 rubles. It checks up on how it has been used. Last year, for example, it found there was not enough money allocated for the social security budget (handling items that do not come under trade union supervision), so it arranged for the transfer of additional funds from other areas. The members of this commission try to find ways to increase the income, and search out new resources, since there are always additional requirements for the welfare of the people of the city.

The Industrial Commission deals with municipal industry, that is, local industry serving the needs of the people directly. It checks on production plans, makes changes in accordance with the requests of the people, always trying to make sure that all enterprises meet the people's needs more fully. Last year, for example, the commission recommended that one of the clothing factories produce a larger proportion of clothing for children and less for adults. The commission members have the right to inspect any enterprise and to invite directors to come before them for questioning. If they find an enterprise badly handled, they can insist that changes be made and if their

---

* As explained earlier, the departments are manned mostly by a paid, professional staff of city employees. The standing commissions, headed by deputies and manned by unpaid volunteer workers, are the main avenue of drawing the general public into volunteer work with the Soviets.

recommendations are not followed, they can insist on the dismissal of the director or anyone in an administrative position. On this commission are competent public figures with important posts in some economic field who volunteer a certain amount of time and also retired professional people who give full time.

The Housing Commission looks after the 10.2 million square meters of housing that is state property. It checks up on the upkeep and repair of apartments and decides on what capital repairs are necessary. In view of the many reports by foreign visitors of the bad state of repair often found in Soviet apartment houses, Yermolovich's words on this are worth quoting directly:

"Now even though this is a socialist country," he told me, "and therefore the welfare of the people is our most basic concern, I must say frankly that there is often carelessness in the matter of capital repairs both in getting them done in time and in their quality. The main city Housing Commission is trying to correct this situation. It has asked the housing commissions of all the District Soviets to pay special attention to the quality of the repairs."

This commission also has to look after small immediate repairs and see that funds, materials and labor are provided. Here too there has been much sloppiness and people have a hard time getting their needs attended to promptly and efficiently. The commission tries to correct this by helping the apartment houses organize their own repair committees made up of skilled people of different trades —plumbers, electricians, etc.—who carry out emergency repairs on a volunteer, mutual aid basis. The city provides whatever tools, materials and so on that are needed.

The Building Commission looks after the actual construction of new apartment houses, hospitals, schools, kindergartens, day nurseries, all kinds of social institutions. Housing is at the very center of the commission's attention. Before 1941, the city covered 4.3 million square meters of living space. Of this, over 1,500,000 square meters was destroyed during the Nazi occupation. That has all been restored, which often meant complete rebuilding, and another 5 million square meters of housing and other building has been added. This commission looks after the proper use of funds and the speed and quality of new construction. Here too there have been serious problems in the past, when quality of building has been sacrificed to speed and quantity. Now that emergency needs have been taken care of, special attention is being paid to quality.

Health, Social Security, Education

THE HEALTH and Social Security Commission has an enormous job helping the regular paid staff of the Soviet's corresponding department. It helps administer the 26 per cent of the city's budget that goes for health needs. The city has seventy-five hospitals and polyclinics with 18,000 beds. About 30,000 people work in its health system. For every 10,000 of the population there are 82 fully qualified doctors. (The United States in 1961 had 142; however, the USSR, as other European countries, utilizes many more trained medical assistants who are not full-fledged doctors than we do, and numerous midwives.) In the outskirts of the city are 39 sanitariums, rest homes and prophylactoria (where workers still on the job who may be getting run down may go at night for special preventive or curative treatment, diet etc.); there are also 147 Young Pioneers' camps and other special institutions that contribute to the people's health.

This commission makes sure that medical care for the whole city is sufficient and timely, that all cases needing immediate attention are taken care of promptly and also looks after prophylactic, preventive measures. The members must make sure that sanitary requirements are met for the city as a whole, that the water supply is biologically clean with no chemicals added, that sanitary norms are observed in restaurants, schools, hospitals, housing. They work with the trade unions to make sure minimum sanitary requirements are provided in all industrial enterprises, and proper measures taken for labor protection and technical safety. ("By the way," the deputy mayor added here, "we have the lowest rate of industrial accidents in the world here in the Ukraine.") The commission has fully qualified specialists in all these fields doing volunteer work for it, and has full rights of inspection, calling in people for questioning, etc.

There had been complaints that a certain polyclinic in Kiev wasn't functioning properly. The commission organized a special doctors' group to work with it on the problem. The doctors carried on an investigation of the polyclinic, personally observing the work of the doctors and staff members, questioning patients, checking up on complaints. Several recommendations were acted on and the necessary changes were made.

The Social Security division of this same commission looks after 150,000 pensioners, makes sure everyone eligible receives their payments, provides whatever help necessary for those who need extra support. Some of the pensioners are war invalids. The commission helps find work for those who are capable of it, trains disabled veterans in special skills, helps them form cooperatives, provides proper housing when needed. Again, a direct quote from Yermolovich:

"We have in our city two special homes, one for invalids, one for pensioners, with 450 places in each. The residents receive free four meals a day and all the clothing they need for summer and winter, from underwear to fur caps. They have lectures on many themes, cultural activities, film showings twice a week. The Institute of Longevity does special work here, applying its latest methods and discoveries.

"I don't like to boast, but I believe that our House of Invalids

34

is the finest in the whole Soviet Union. Specialists from all over the country and from many other countries as well, including the United States, have been here to visit it. It is situated in the Belostino Microdistrict,* a very pleasant locality, where there is much greenery."

The Commission on Public Education looks after the city's 29 schools, with about 250,000 pupils. Education, as everywhere in the USSR, is obligatory through eight years, and there is no longer any illiteracy in the Ukraine. Every fourth person in the Republic is a student either at a primary, secondary or higher educational establishment. The commission checks up on fulfillment of the school plan, on school buildings and equipment and on the calibre of the teaching. Last winter on the commission's insistence a new school was built in one of Kiev's microdistricts.

The commission also pays much attention to extra-curricular work, the work of the Parent-Teacher Committees, organization of proper rest and recreation for children during vacations, etc. There are also in the city 28 higher educational institutions, with some 63,000 students, 68 technical schools, a Ukrainian Academy of Sciences which the commission helps in various ways.

Volunteers for Beautifying Kiev and Improving Services

THE COMMISSION for Improving Park Services and Greenery ... We were all three getting pretty exhausted by this time. My notes were becoming rather unintelligible, Asya's voice was only a whisper, Yermolovich himself was growing hoarse. But now he suddenly took on a new animation and his eyes lit up, as he said:

"Our Kiev is very fond of greenery! We keep planting more trees and shrubbery and flowers every year. We now have 76,000 hectares of greenery, that's more than Paris, Warsaw, Moscow, Leningrad, Rome or London [or even New York, I murmured]. That means we have 18.5 square meters of greenery for every person, or if we consider all the environs, we have 326 square meters per person, the highest in the world. The figures I have here give 8.5 square meters per person in New York, 5.3 for London, 11 for Paris. We have 25 big recreation parks, 174 city squares full of greenery and trees, as you can see, line all our streets.

"In all the new microdistricts we need much greenery, for every new area opened up has to live up to the general amount of greenery in the city. In addition to looking after what we already have, the volunteers on this commission take part in projecting new public parks, new 'green masses.' Everything must be landscaped in accordance with the general contours of the city. In planting new beds of flowers, harmonious colors must be carefully worked out; we want nothing garish, not too formal, everything simple and beautiful.

---

* Microdistrict is the term used in the Soviet Union for new self-sufficient housing projects with their own stores, schools, hospitals, etc., so that all community services are within easy reach of the residents.

Argument at Zaporozhye City Soviet: Dr. Liudmila Petrova (right), a deputy, speaks of need to pave a new road. Deputy Ivan Kachan, Finance Department head, says too much money is already being spent on roads.

"All this needs a great deal of care—landscaping, agro-technical measures, watering, weeding, tree surgery. Many specialists volunteer their services for this commission.

"We call this our Green City of Lime and Chestnut Trees. You've seen our chestnut trees in bloom in the spring? [Oh yes, I had!] We are especially proud of our chestnut trees. Now our scientists and tree specialists are planning to introduce some new types of trees replacing old ones which are not attractive and only make the city dirty with their dropping pods, with more of our Ukrainian national tree, the chestnut. In addition to the horse chestnuts which are merely decorative, we are also planning to plant some real chestnut trees on the outskirts of the city. Then we must also look after the vertical greenery on all our hills. We want every part of our city to be decorative and beautiful. The commission calls on our landscape gardeners for help in this."

Next, the Commission on Trade and Public Catering. This commission's duty is to check on the food supplies in the city's 4,000 trade enterprises, stores, restaurants, etc., including supplies both from government purchases from state and collective farms and from the collective farmer's private plots. In the past five years Kiev's trade turnover had multiplied 27 times. The standard of living was rising, and the population was buying more TVs, refrigerators, washing machines, pianos and other musical instruments. Efforts were being made to bring the supplies of consumers' goods closer to the needs of the people, and to improve service to customers in the shops.

I quote Yermolovich's own words again at this point:

"Naturally, if we could only be sure we would not have to defend our country again in a war and didn't have to spend so much on arms, we would have the possibility of supplying all the peoples' needs. You can see all around you that we are building, building, building. We want to keep on building, to make sure that no one will interfere with this and that all we are building will not be destroyed again in another war."

The Commission on Transport and Communications. Yermolovich's voice had grown hoarser, my poor little Asya's voice had practically vanished, she looked at me pleadingly, but Yermolovich kept doggedly on. We were still only at the ninth commission out of 14! The city was growing so fast, transportation couldn't keep up with it. This commission had to work out how many people had to be transported each day at rush hours and other times, by bus, street car, metro and rail. Billions of rubles in freight go through Kiev daily by rail and truck. Additional roads needed to be built so these could by-pass the city. A circular electric railroad is being built around the city to ease the passenger load on other forms of transportation. Streets need to be widened. The problems are immense! Telephone communications must be improved. Still another commission is at work on coordinating all the transportation services.

At commission No. 11, on Communal Services to the Population, we all collapsed. The reader will have to use his own imagination applying the principles and practices already described, to figure out how the remaining commissions work. The title "Commission on City Planning" is self-explanatory. One of its main concerns is to avoid air and water pollution. The Cultural Commission has to do with all theaters, orchestras, cinema, palaces of culture, clubs of all kinds. The Commission on Socialist Law and Legality, considered one of the most important of all, checks the work of all administrative organs to guard against violations of Soviet law and also checks on such peoples' organs as the Comradely Courts and the People's Volunteer Public Order Squads.

But Boris Feodorovich, himself almost voiceless now, still had a few things he wanted to say about his beloved city and all the things that were being done to make it more beautiful and more comfortable by both the government and the people themselves. His final words, reminiscent of Miranda's "Oh Brave New World!" in *The Tempest*, were:

"This is a good city—there are wonderful people in it!"

Chapter 4

A DISTRICT SOVIET IN MOSCOW

MY LAST week back in Moscow, following the visit to Kiev and its City Soviet described in the previous section, came during preparations for the 1964 November anniversary celebration.

With the whole city involved in the festivities of this main national holiday, it was almost impossible to make appointments, so I was especially grateful that the officials of the Leningrad District Soviet of Moscow should take the time for an interview.

Chairman Scherbakov, courteous and handsome, received me in the reception room of the modern District Soviet building on Leningrad Chaussée. He introduced me to Comrade Shubin, first deputy chairman; Comrade Malkova, a woman official, "Our moneybags," he quipped (she headed the financial department); Comrade Lavrienko, head of the Department on General Questions; and Barinova, another woman official, chief inspector of the Soviet. Others joined us later at the long green-baize covered table.

While coffee and cakes and fruit were pressed upon me, Comrade Scherbakov told the others about the work of *New World Review*. Then he picked up a pointer and turning to a chart of the organization of the Soviet on a stand beside him, said in a business-like way:

"I have been told by the representative of the Friendship Committee that you are seeking information about how our District Soviet functions, and how the people of our city take part in our work as volunteers. Now tell us, please, what would you like to know?"

"Everything!" I said.

"Very well, I will do my best," he said, not batting an eye. "I shall, if you will permit be, assume the role of school teacher."

He began with a description of Leningrad District. One of Moscow's thirteen districts, with a population of half a million, it encompasses practically every phase of the life of the Soviet capital. It is an industrial district, with both heavy and light industry; a center of science and culture with many higher education and scientific research institutes, two theaters, numerous cinemas and clubs and other cultural institutions. It is an air and water transportation center, encompassing the Sheremetovo Airport, which links Moscow with many foreign countries, and the Khimki Reservoir and Northern Port of the big canal system connecting the Black and Caspian Seas with the Baltic, through which sea-going vessels now come to Moscow. It is a sport center, with water sports on the reservoir and canals and indoor swimming pools, and land sports with facilities in two large stadiums, several Young Pioneers' sport grounds and extensive park recreation zones. It is a center of new housing, with a quarter of a million meters of new housing space already built during the past year along with schools, kindergartens, day nurseries, restaurants, dry cleaning establishments, beauty parlors and all sorts of other communal services which are now a part of the new self-contained "microdistricts."

He then gave me a detailed account of the functioning of their District Soviet of 250 deputies, one for each 2,500 of the population. About half of the deputies are women, and half are party members, half non-party. It soon became apparent that in a large city like Moscow a District Soviet is actually in charge of a whole city in itself, so its functions differed little from that of the City Soviet in other places I had visited. I shall repeat here only the things I learned that add something to what I have already recorded.

Scherbakov explained the relation between the City Soviet and the District Soviets in this way:

"The organization of the District Soviet in general follows that of the City Soviet except that in certain cases the City Soviet has functions lacking in the District Soviet. For example, the City Soviet has a department dealing with the architecture and planning of construction on a citywide scale. The District Soviet has only a volunteer architectural and city planning committee, which finds out the needs of the district and brings them before the City Soviet, thus helping to coordinate the needs of the district with those of the city as a whole."

He went on to tell me that the City Soviet has both an Industrial Department and an Industrial Standing Commission, because the City Soviet has a large number of industrial enterprises under its jurisdiction; there is no such department or commission in the District Soviet. The Financial and Budget Department and Commission deal with industrial enterprises in the district, because part of the turnover tax from state industrial enterprises goes to the district to help finance its undertakings.

The work of the District Soviet is coordinated with that of the City Soviet through Deputies' Councils. Formed at the first session of the Soviets after elections, the councils are made up of seven to twelve Deputies from both the City and District Soviets living in a given area. All microdistricts have such Deputies' Councils, which deal directly with questions connected with the life and work of the people. They are also formed to serve a specific educational area or economic unit. Through these Deputies' Councils the work of all the District Soviet departments and standing commissions are coordinated with that of the City Soviet.

The Deputies' Councils check up on matters of housing, trade, restaurants, cultural and health agencies. They direct or coordinate the work of social organizations in the area, make recommendations on apartment allocation, help the Standing Commissions in their organizational work, help implement the demands of the electors, and so on. They do not act as Soviets in themselves and have no legislative or administrative powers, only advisory functions. Yet they seem to have considerable authority, and being directly on the spot manage to get a lot of things attended to.

The departments of the District Soviet, and the Standing Commissions described by Scherbakov, corresponded very closely with those of the Kiev Soviet. The Departments were staffed with professional workers, while the Standing Commissions were the main means of involving the people directly in the work of self-government, in a wholly volunteer capacity. Yet it was clear that there was no hidebound organizational form, but that differences occurred from Republic to Republic and from city to city to meet local needs.

One difference was that whereas in Kiev questions of social Welfare and Health were combined in one Standing Commission, here they had to have a separate one on social welfare, since there were 74,000 pensioners in the district with other problems than those of health. About 32 million rubles were paid out to these pensioners annually, and some received additional bonuses. One function of the Social Welfare Commission was to give personal attention to making sure that all pensioners received the money due to them, the free care in sanitariums to which they were entitled, proper housing, and other matters. But the main question for many pensioners was that they wanted to go on functioning rather than to retire. Joining the volunteer "activ" of the Standing Commissions offered the best solution. Here they could go on working in their professions either full or part time in accordance with their strength: retired doctors and nurses with the Health Commission, teachers with the Education Commission, people of the arts with the Cultural Commission, and the like.

The Soviet and Socialist Legality

SCHERBAKOV emphasized the importance of the Standing Commission on Socialist Law and Legality. Although the regular People's Courts, the Procurator's office, the militia and other organizations and agencies of the legal and police system do not come directly under the supervision of the Soviet, the chairmen of the

People's Courts within their district must be approved by the Soviet. It is the responsibility of this legal commission to check into the operation of the courts and militia in their district and immediately report back to the Soviet *Ispolkom* (Executive Committee) if they find any violations of Soviet law, any cases of injustice in the People's Courts or any incorrect behavior on the part of the militia.

There are certain Administrative Committees directly under the *Ispolkom* which have limited powers, as for example calling to account or dismissing any house manager or other person violating any rules of sanitation or public order. The Standing Commission on Law checks up on the work of such Committees, reports to them when action is needed and investigates measures taken. Complaints may be brought to this Commission by any citizen of the District.

The Standing Commission on Socialist Law and Legality also checks up on the work of such people's organizations as the Comradely Courts and the People's Volunteer Public Order Squads, which now handle cases of minor law infringement formerly taken care of by the People's Courts and the militia. It looks into the handling of cases where persons found guilty of minor offenses are paroled in the care of some public group instead of being sentenced to prison.

"In these days," Scherbakov told me, "we guard our socialist legality like the apple of our eye. We must make sure that we never again have the violations of laws and arbitrary arrests and punishments that existed in the past. While we must protect society against the actions of criminals, we must also protect the rights of every Soviet citizen. The main job of course is to do away with crime altogether, to build the kind of life for people that will make crimes unthinkable to them."

The Work of Volunteers

I LEARNED that while a great deal was being done in Moscow, as everywhere else, in drawing people into volunteer work (this District Soviet had 25,000 regular volunteers), the size of the city and the complexity of the organization of life required that there be some paid workers in the Standing Commissions. The Cultural Commission, for example, acting in close contact with the Department of Culture, had two paid workers in addition to 700 active volunteer workers.

There is an immense amount of cultural activity in the district, which has 116 Houses of Culture, clubs, cinemas, music schools and some 75 recreation rooms. The Cultural Commission keeps an eye on their work to make sure their needs are taken care of. The Commission also cooperates with *Znanye,* another of the public organizations that has taken over work formerly handled under government supervision. It is an outgrowth of the former "All Union Society for the Dissemination of Knowledge." Now it's just called "Knowledge" and organizes lectures on every subject under the sun that people are interested in or that government and party leaders think they should be interested in—whether current affairs, space travel, hygiene, organized literary circles among the tenants, librarians who set up some aspect of culture or, very frequently, an immediate burning issue like the war in Vietnam.

Special smaller volunteer councils look after many supplementary cultural projects which are always springing up, such as organizing exhibitions, discussion groups on some community problem or artistic activity. It is up to the Soviet to help find premises for such purposes.

There are many opportunities for amateur cultural activities in the workers' and pioneer clubs and in the schools. But there are still many people who are not drawn in, and these supplementary apartment house and block activities are important means of helping to bring out the creative potential of some who might otherwise stay aloof, and in providing worthwhile leisure time activities.

Questions of Culture and Recreation

IN THIS, as in other District Soviets, the Housing Commission and the Cultural Commission cooperate in measures for culture and recreation and use of leisure time. They work with the tenants' committees in converting whatever area is available around the apartment houses or in the courtyard space around which they are built into gardens and play areas. Architects living there help draw up plans, artists and sculptors contribute their gifts to making them more attractive. Instances were cited of former teachers who organized societies of booklovers, debating centers at libraries, special reading circles for children and meetings of writers and readers.

Artists in apartment houses in the area organize special art classes for children, and adults too, and an opera singer helped organize choral groups. Outside professional help was called in to help in the development of amateur circles of various kinds. The Art Theater and the Mali Theater provided personnel to help set up drama circles, the Bolshoy Ballet company furnished teachers for ballet circles, the Artists' Union provided teachers for art classes. In one district the Composers' Union set up a People's Music University. Dancing in the parks was organized for the summer months, with volunteer bands from the district.

This district possessed large stadiums and other sport facilities. The Sport Commission of the District Soviet also arranged for block soccer and ice hockey teams of both young and old.

There had been some sharp criticism of the young people of Moscow for not helping enough in volunteer community activities. I myself had noticed several articles in the press urging that the Komsomols pay more attention to community activities rather than confining themselves to the factories or other institutions on which their organization was based. The District Soviet was working on this problem, too.

This District Soviet felt that it was not yet ready to replace any of the regular Soviet departments with commissions as was already being done in some places, although there was now a tendency to put some of the regular *Ispolkom* Departments themselves on a public, voluntary basis. Draft resolutions are circulated widely in advance of meetings to insure discussion and mobilize volunteers.

"The question has already arisen," Scherbakov told me, "of drawing more and more activists to work on a volunteer basis in the departments as well as the commissions, which opens the way to their merging later on. We already have many activists who come to the departments as well as to the commissions on a regular daily basis, arriving in the morning and spending the day, or a large part of it. Some of them are pensioners, some housewives who haven't regular jobs outside the home, sometimes they are workers on night shifts who want to fill up part of the day with some other activity.

"There are some aspects of our work that people find very exciting. For example, we have a special department examining letters and complaints from the people which is very popular and entirely manned by volunteers. People like to feel that they are taking an active part in righting wrongs, the volunteers are very useful in finding out the actual facts for us and checking on whether complaints are justified and in working out what's to be done about it.

"We also have certain committees attached to the Soviets that are neither departments or commissions, but have specialized tasks which many activists are drawn into. There is such a committee supervising the activities of the Comradely Courts, another supervising the work of apartment house management and still another checking the use of our housing funds and making sure there are no injustices in the distribution."

This reminded me of an instance of such a special committee I had seen in the beautiful little city of Sumgait, outside of Baku, capital of Azerbaidzhan. There was a special Art Committee attached to the Sumgait Soviet. They had nothing to do with the planning, architecture and building of the town; their only task was to do anything they could to add to the beauty of the town in small ways. The Sumgait street lamps were of modern design, and unusually decorative. When I remarked on them, I learned that one of the members of the Art Committee had seen such lamps on a visit to Cuba, and brought back the design to be copied for Sumgait. The Art Committee had also seen to it that the park benches scattered around the city were painted attractive colors and had helped in the interior decorating of a new movie theater, the Youth Club and other buildings.

When I mentioned this, Scherbakov told me that similar activities were carried on through the District Soviet's Cultural Commission. However, he said, he had heard that a number of City Soviets throughout the country had set up special commissions "to do away with everything that is vulgar and in bad taste and to introduce beauty into daily life," and that this too was the purpose of their own cultural workers.

The District Soviet and Housing

AGAIN AND again Scherbakov came back to the question of housing as the main concern of the District Soviet. The district had three and a half million square meters of housing space, 55 per cent under the supervision of the Soviet, the remainder built by various factories, plants or other enterprises. Only about one per cent of the housing in this district was in private, individual houses. Just a few rather tumbledown old houses still remained in what used to be the village of Khimka, where the port now is. These were being gradually demolished and the people being moved into new houses. The District Soviet always made sure that new housing was ready and that the people agreed to move before any demolition was undertaken.

The Housing Department of the Soviet had eighteen paid workers on its staff, and they could not possibly deal with all the matters involved in the distribution of thousands of apartments (12,000 new ones ready for habitation each year). So in addition to the regular staff there are 32 activists connected with the Department working out of their main office and 250 others working in the apartment houses in cooperation with the management. They visit families personally and find out about their problems, so they know the needs of the population better than the paid staff members of the Housing Department. They consider individual requests for apartments, check up on conditions, record apartments that become available, and try to have them allocated to the most needy. Tenants' meetings are called frequently with notices posted in advance, urging everyone to come and to make known their complaints and suggestions.

Among other ways in which this and other District Soviets in Moscow helped look after the tenants' needs and to encourage volunteers activities of the tenants themselves, was to arrange that a certain percentage of the money received in rent be placed in the hands of the tenants' committees for the special needs of their housing units or blocks. When this was not sufficient, they or the tenants found additional funds, by arranging exhibits or performances and charging a small entrance fee for example.

Art exhibits were a favorite way of doing this. One night when we were strolling around Moscow we saw a huge crowd surging into an apartment house. We discovered that this was the last night of an exhibit arranged by several young artists in the area. The crowd was too great for us to get in, and they were in process of closing the exhibit in any case. From comments we heard and tantalizing glimpses through the windows, we gathered that some of the work shown, both in sculpture and painting, was of the abstract kind frowned on by the authorities. There were hot arguments going on among the partisans and the critics of avant garde art, but there had been no official interference with the holding of such an exhibition.

Deputy Chairman Shubin said he would like to add something on the kind of mutual aid the people were engaged in, in matters which they formerly had to refer to the apartment house management or the corresponding Department of the Soviet, often involving much red tape and delay. It appeared that the system here was similar to that in Kiev described previously. Capital repairs were taken care of through the Soviet.

"But for smaller problems," Shubin said, "we have about 500 'repair *druzhini*' (volunteer work squads would be the best translation, not of course to be confused with the people's volunteer public order squads, which are also called *druzhini*). These groups of 'repair *druzhini*' are formed by the tenants themselves. Skilled workers of various specialties volunteer at a general tenants meeting and form the *druzhini* who do the repairs for the tenants. They look after keeping plumbing, heating, water supply, electricity and so on in order. Each member gives about five hours of volunteer work monthly. The principle is 'Scratch my back and I'll scratch yours!' For example, a plasterer will help an electrician and another day the plasterer will need the electrician. A painter may help a plumber and vice versa. Instruments, tools, building materials, parts and equipment are all guaranteed by the Soviet. But the labor itself is given freely.

"Professional people also take part in this mutual aid. Doctors volunteer for duty for certain hours in the Red Corners (apartment house clubs), examine patients for minor ailments in their spare .time, either applying the immediate remedy or arranging for a trip to a clinic or hospital if necessary. A special Volunteer Medical Council of experienced doctors and medical scientists assists our Health Department, conducts courses.

"Actors and musicians give their services for an evening of entertainment—everyone contributes something of his own special skills or gifts.

"Our Soviet was saved tens of thousands of rubles through such volunteer work. And the people were saved the frustration of endless calls to the management or the Soviet and endless waiting before things got done.

"But the material side, the economy, is only part of it. Such

45

measures are also an important means of Communist education, of increasing the spirit of mutual aid among the people. Many new friendships are made in this way.

"Another aspect of all this is that when the tenants repair things with their own hands, they become more careful and keep things in better condition than when they depend on some anonymous person outside. They develop pride of workmanship. They do not want to be bawled out by their neighbors for sloppy work.

"This work is all done on an organized basis. The chief engineer and technician of the house management keep track of what needs to be done and where and when and by whom. All those who participate keep careful record of the time spent, the materials used, and so on. These few hours given each month do not appear to be too great burden on anyone. And it is really very heartening to see the amount of public spirit generated in this way."

Children Are Very Important People

LAVRIENKO, a woman official, told of work with children: "We also have some kindergartens that are run on a volunteer basis. In general we try to provide kindergartens for all children whose mothers want them, but still only about 20 to 25 per cent of our children are taken care of in regular kindergartens. Some of our mothers, strange as it may seem in this day and age, still prefer the 'nanny' system. If the wife's mother or mother-in-law lives with them—and that's too often the case—the mother will often depend on granny to take care of the child. But there are always mothers who find difficulty in getting their children into kindergartens because there are not enough places. So when we learn that there isn't enough kindergarten space, our first job is to try to get more kindergartens built. Meantime, we bridge the gap by finding the necessary premises through the Soviet and our Standing Commissions help us find volunteer nurses, cooks and attendants. These volunteers are usually pensioners, housewives, retired doctors and nurses."

Might not this mean, I asked, that there would be too elderly a group in charge of the children?

"Oh no," she answered, "we are very careful about that. First we make sure that personnel in the kindergarten are fond of children and experienced in working with them. Then we always have on the staff, doing practice work under the supervision of the older people, students of the pedagogical or medical or musical institutes—for music is one of the most important things in working with children. Don't worry, there are always plenty of young people around!

"For example the first voluntary nursery school, on 2nd Peschannaya Street was organized by Vera Lavrova, a pensioned teacher. Fifty-seven students of the Lenin Teachers' Institute do practice work there regularly on a rotation system. The children are taught music, the rudiments of English. A doctor living in the same block of apartments looks after their health. The tenants on the block have seen to it that the walls are attractively papered, and furniture provided and kept in repair. Older children from the neighborhood make the toys and some of the equipment in their school shop.

"In general," she went on, "we do a great deal of work both for the children and the young people of our district. To us they are very important people. We have, for example, a special 'children's highway' in our district, which no one else may use. The children love it! We have specially built small cars which they are taught to drive by well qualified instructors, and when they pass all the necessary tests—which are very strict, as with all our drivers—they receive 'young drivers' licenses."

Lavrienko explained to me that this project, taken care of by the Young Pioneers, was run entirely by the pupils of the fifth to seventh grades, under adult supervision, but with children carrying the main responsibility. It had been found that special interest in technical matters and the craze about auto driving is practically universal among children of 12-14. Later, there begins to be a differentiation of interest. But knowledge of cars and their motors is useful no matter what they do, and this practice helps in carrying out the principles of polytechnical education.

Training classes for the children are held in a special building, and the cars, garages and all the necessary equipment are provided by the Soviet. The children learn all about the motor and its care, the construction of the automobile and how to drive and repair it. Models of the whole mechanism are provided for them to learn on. They are also taught traffic rules. On the children's highway actual traffic conditions are simulated while all necessary measures are taken to insure the children's safety. The children also direct traffic. They hold administrative positions as chief of the project, chief of the garage, chief of servicing and repair. A children's council, with adult advisors, is in overall charge.

"Children need heroes, people to look up to. So we make a special point of finding out people who are doing especially interesting things who live in our district, and putting the children in touch with them. We always get wonderful cooperation from such people. It is a big thrill to the children to find out that some important writer or artist or explorer or spaceman like Gagarin is a next door neighbor!"

THE officials of this Moscow District Soviet, as all the others I had interviewed, emphasized the importance of maintaining close contacts between the deputies and their electors. During election campaigns the voters are requested to submit their suggestions and complaints to the district election commissioners.

STRUCTURAL SET-UP OF MOSCOW CITY

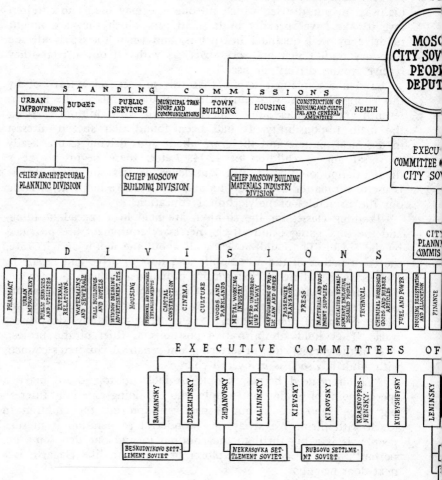

MOSCOW CITY SOVIET OF PEOPLE'S DEPUTIES

S T A N D I N G   C O M M I S S I O N S

URBAN IMPROVEMENT	BUDGET	PUBLIC SERVICES	MUNICIPAL TRANSPORT AND COMMUNICATIONS	TOWN BUILDING	HOUSING	CONSTRUCTION OF HOUSING AND CULTURAL AND GENERAL AMENITIES	HEALTH

EXECUTIVE COMMITTEE OF CITY SOVIET

CHIEF ARCHITECTURAL PLANNING DIVISION

CHIEF MOSCOW BUILDING DIVISION

CHIEF MOSCOW BUILDING MATERIALS INDUSTRY DIVISION

CITY PLANNING COMMISSION

D I V I S I O N S

- PHARMACY
- URBAN IMPROVEMENT
- PUBLIC SERVICES AND UTILITIES
- EXTERNAL RELATIONS
- WATERMAINS AND SEWERAGE
- TALL BUILDINGS AND HOTELS
- WINDOW DRESSING, ADVERTISEMENT, ETC.
- HOUSING
- PERSONNEL AND EDUCATIONAL ESTABLISHMENTS
- CAPITAL CONSTRUCTION
- CINEMA
- CULTURE
- WOODS AND PARKLANDS
- METAL WORKING INDUSTRY
- METRO UNDERGROUND RAILWAY
- SAFEGUARDING OF PUBLIC LAW AND ORDER
- PASSENGER TRANSPORT
- PRESS
- MATERIALS AND EQUIPMENT SUPPLIES
- SPECIALIZED ESTABLISHMENTS EMPLOYING DISABLED PEOPLE
- TECHNICAL
- CHEMICAL HOUSEHOLD GOODS AND RUBBER ARTICLES
- FUEL AND POWER
- HOUSING REGISTRATION AND ALLOCATION
- FINANCE

E X E C U T I V E   C O M M I T T E E S   O F

- BAUMANSKY
- DZERZHINSKY
- ZHDANOVSKY
- KALININSKY
- KIEVSKY
- KIROVSKY
- KRASNOPRESNENSKY.
- KUIBYSHEVSKY
- LENINSKY

BESKUDNIKOVO SETTLEMENT SOVIET

NEKRASOVKA SETTLEMENT SOVIET

RUBLOVO SETTLEMENT SOVIET

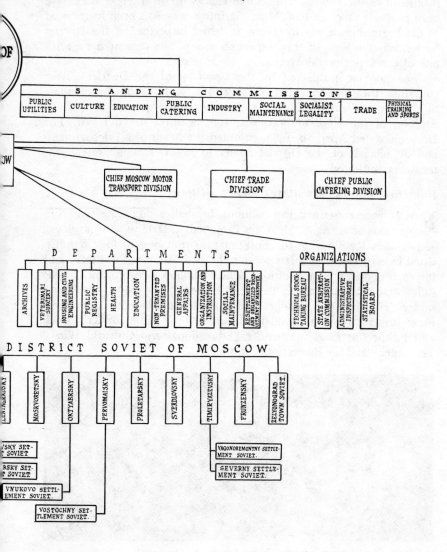

Voters are encouraged to bring their complaints and requests to the deputies at all times. But a special point is made of bringing their needs before the candidates for deputies in the election period.

The voters' requests and complaints are printed in a booklet of which every deputy has a copy, since all must share the responsibility of carrying out the will of the voters. In addition, a special inspection team set up under the *Ispolkom* (Executive Committee) supervises the fulfilment of the voters' requests and checks up on whether they have been properly taken care of. Mme. Barinova, who had been introduced at the beginning of our interview as "chief inspector" of the District Soviet, was the head of this inspection group. She presented me with one of the deputies' booklets.

The booklet, published by the *Ispolkom* of the District Soviet, contained the complete plan of "measures for fulfilling the mandate of the electors," in the March 3, 1963 elections, and the text of the decision of the *Ispolkom* ratifying the measures to be taken. The Decision, dated April 10, 1963, enjoined the heads of all departments and all officials of the District Soviet to follow through on all the measures indicated.

How the Voters' Mandates Are Fulfilled

EACH page contained five columns, headed: 1. Mandates and Suggestions of voters; 2. Measures Proposed; 3. Date to be Completed; 4. Deputies Responsible for Fulfillment (from one to four deputies listed in each case). The last column, headed "Results," was left blank for each deputy's own notations. The mandates were grouped under different headings. Under "Public Welfare," 25 requests were listed; under "Housing," 38; under "Communal and Household Services," nine; under "Transport and Communications," nine; under "Trade and Public Catering," 34; under "Educational and Cultural Work," 14; under "Health Protection," nine.

Dmitri Shostakovich, famous Soviet composer, meets with voters during his campaign for deputy to the Council of Nationalities of the Supreme Soviet. He was elected.

Here are some of the decisions taken on carrying out the voters' requests. To see that dust-collecting apparatus is installed in the "Izolyator" and "Yava" factories. To close Ussilevich Street #2 to traffic because it's too narrow and a school is located there. To prohibit trucks going through the courtyard of #34 Skakova Street where there are always a lot of children playing. To pave the entryway to Kindergarten #43, which now gets too muddy. To install more lights on a dimly-lighted street, to regulate the water supply in a certain apartment house, to finish repairs on another, with attention to the quality, to mend the roof and repair the cracks in another, and many similar requests. To eliminate a section of the road to the airport which is too close to some apartment houses and very noisy. To save a certain birch grove and turn it into a park of rest and recreation for the workers nearby.

Under housing, to see that a Housing Administration office is installed in the apartment house on Bolshoy Kopetevsky, since the tenants now have to go one to five kilometers away. To set up a special committee of Old Bolsheviks to make sure that housing space is properly distributed. To look after questions of heat, water supply, electricity, repairs and garbage removal in certain designated houses. To find other apartments for families living in the student dormitories in the "Sokol" area who have nothing to do with the higher educational institutions to which the dormitories are attached. To provide club rooms in certain apartments lacking them. To do something about the noise of the "technological machinery" in the cafe "Cheburechnaya" because its 24-hour uproar has made life in apartment house #58 on Leningrad Clausee "absolutely impossible." (The solution was the installation of noiseless machinery.) To find new quarters for the people who live in No. 13-15 Second Airport Proyezd, which are really only barracks not fit for habitation. (Current repairs to be done pending the finding of new homes for these people and the demolition of the barracks.) To find new homes for certain families living in the basements of decrepit old houses, moving out families with children first (a whole series of requests have to do with moving families from unfit quarters).

Under communal and household services were such requests and decisions as enlargement of a certain public bathhouse, opening a mending shop for knitted goods, opening barber shops, beauty parlors, shoe repair, tailoring, dressmaking and mending and dry cleaning and laundry establishments. Under transport and communications, decisions on increasing the number of trolleys and autobuses, improving transportation to outlying sections, installing more public telephones, changing the route of a trolley line "in order to provide relative peace and quiet for the workers living in apartment houses on Volokolamsk Chausee."

On trade, to take measures to improve the services in provision store No. 69 on Raskova Street "where it is usually dirty and uncomfortable, with many drunks around, and the salespeople are rude." To open a department store in another section having none nearby. To add a department of semi-prepared foods to a certain restaurant. To open a new vegetable and fruit store in one section, keep another open for longer hours, and to see that vegetable storage is handled better, since sometimes vegetables on sale are in poor condition. (A whole series of requests for more vegetable and fruit stores.) To improve dairy supplies. To increase the number of produce stores on the left side of Leningrad Prospekt. To open a dietetic restaurant in Airport Proyezd. More demands to open departments of semi-prepared foods. To open another newsstand. To improve the work of a certain bakery.

In the sphere of education and culture, to improve the equipment of a certain kindergarten; to organize a youth club; to complete a certain park; to improve mass cultural work and establish a House of Culture in Khoroshevsky Microdistrict; to install playground equipment for children in a certain park; to establish a new library and reading room in the Kosmodemiansky Microdistrict. To build a new school in another microdistrict—and more libraries and more parks and more playgrounds and more clubs—all to be established or looked into.

On health—to improve the health services in a number of medical institutions, to increase the number of polyclinics, to open a new dental clinic, to enlarge a certain drug store, to improve the children's polyclinic in one of the microdistricts.

In some cases, it was noted that the recommended measures had been taken immediately. Running through the booklet, Chairman Scherbakov told me that practically every measure scheduled to be completed in 1963 had already been taken care of, and most of those scheduled for completion in 1964 were under way. In only a few places had there been a collective decision that certain measures requested and proposed had been found unpractical. One of the items followed by the terse word "inexpedient" was the request to "put a stop to the sale of wine and vodka products at Shop No. 5 on Nizhnie Street."

Some Criticisms from Within

THE Soviets I visited were probably among the better organized and more efficient. I have no doubt at all that I would have heard similar accounts in many many other places. Casual meetings here and there around the country with people working either as Soviet deputies or as volunteers all filled in and confirmed the general picture that had been given me.

At the same time, I am sure the situation is very uneven, that there are places not nearly as successful as those I have written about in meeting the voters needs and in drawing in the general population

52

for volunteer work. Indeed, from stories and articles written in the press one often hears of bureaucratic functioning of Soviets, of cut and dried and very formal meetings with only leadership people making long dry reports and very little discussion, of rank and file deputies who wish to speak going unrecognized and many deputies failing to keep close ties with the voters and to report to them regularly, and so on.

An account of some of the negative as well as the positive aspects of the work of the Soviets was written by Ya. Nasriddinova, the remarkable woman who is the Chairman of the Presidium of the Supreme Soviet of Uzbek Soviet Socialist Republic, an office tantamount to President of Uzbekistan. Her article appeared in *Izvestia* (its English text was published in the October 6, 1964 issue of Novosti Press Agency's *Daily Review*).

Nasriddinova wrote of the former practice in her Republic of reports prepared for Soviet sessions by the *Ispolkom,* in which everything was prearranged, with little left for the deputies to do except approve, only one or two taking the floor during discussions.

This, she wrote, was being corrected and Soviet sessions are being made more democratic by omitting entirely any obligatory reports. Instead, draft decisions were circulated among the deputies well in advance of the sessions, providing plenty of time for the deputies to think over the proposals and discuss them with their constituents in preparation for full discussions at the Soviet session. She gave as an example a draft decision on public health conditions circulated by the Chilanzar District Soviet in Tashkent. As a result of preparatory work with public health workers and ordinary citizens a lively and constructive discussion was held which resulted in a decision quite different from the original draft.

Nasriddinova spoke of other District Soviets which made a practice of publishing draft decisions in the local newspapers and broadcasting them over the radio to insure full public participation in their solution. Yet, she said, "more often than not, unfortunately, the people are acquainted neither with the problems which the Soviet will be solving at its regular session nor with the decisions it will adopt."

She also wrote of the very important work being done by the Standing Commissions now that they had been invested with broader powers than formerly. She indicated, however, that there were still too many cases when the Standing Commissions remained merely consultative organs and continued to be deprived of the right to take decisions binding on the Ispolkom and to assume, even partially, administrative functions as they were now supposed to do.

(Only today, while editing this material for publication, I came across an article in the March 11, 1967 *Soviet Weekly,* published by the USSR Embassy in London, by a Deputy to another District Soviet in Moscow, complaining that there are still serious drawbacks in the work of the Standing Committees. He indicates that they do not have sufficient authority and that the question of giving them wider powers, which had presumably been solved back in 1964, is still on the order of the day! This does not mean that what I have written was not true of the Soviets I visited. It means that the *application* of measures strengthening democracy is not always even. What I have described is the goal everywhere, although not everywhere yet achieved.)

Nasriddinova's sharpest criticisms were directed against those deputies, of whom she said there were many in her Republic, who failed to maintain close ties with their electors, who considered their post of deputy as a mere adjunct to whatever official position they held and shunned doing ordinary "spade work." She mentioned as examples a certain Comrade Sharipov, deputy of the Chirchik City Soviet and Secretary of the City Komsomol Committee, who had not been seen by his electors for over a year. Another, Comrade Razhev, deputy manager of a building materials plant at Superfosfatny, had only attended two of the sessions of the Township Soviet, even though he had been elected to its *Ispolkom*. She said in such cases it was necessary to make use of the right of recall and that "we should also call to account the public organizations that nominated these people and then forgot about them."

She expressed great satisfaction in the replacement of 5,000 full-time paid staff workers of Soviets throughout Uzbekistan with volunteers. She praised the work of Khurshida Khudaybergenova, who for many years had headed the *Ispolkom* of the Khiva Town Soviet. This woman mayor carried on her work with only three full-time assistants in her nine departments which, along with the Standing Commissions, all operate on a volunteer basis.

Evidence of volunteer activities in Uzbekistan, similar to those described to me in Kiev and Moscow, is seen in this description by Nasriddinova:

> Block committees and commissions of owners of private homes have become the largest mass organs of self-government in Uzbekistan. They have been set up in Tashkent, Namangan, Fergana, Kokand, Urgench and other cities and towns. Their activities are based on the principle of doing everything on a volunteer basis. They improve public services in their neighborhoods, organize libraries, tea rooms, universities of culture, etc. on volunteer principles. In the Tashkent Oktiabrsky District, 40 shops, health centers, post offices, clubs and tea rooms were built by the population on the initiative of these committees.

Criticism as Prelude to Correction

CERTAIN other negative features of the local Soviets were pointed out in the study of the Soviets of Kazakhstan, previously referred to. This criticism was the prelude to the measures of correcting previous errors and expanding democracy that have been described.

While recognizing the colossal work in strengthening local government agencies conducted during the years 1955 to 1959, the authors say it would be wrong to remain silent about further mistakes made between 1960 and 1964. They write* that the "frequent and unfounded reorganizations of the government machinery occurring until the October (1964) Plenum of the Central Committee of the CPSU (when Khrushchev was removed) had essentially denigrated the role of the Soviets." Measures such as setting up the regional economic organs (*sovnarkhozi*) had artificially narrowed the sphere of activity of local government in the realm of production, limiting them to matters of housing, consumer and socio-cultural services. Confusion had resulted from the division into separate industrial and agricultural zones previously referred to. Sometimes mechanical reduction of paid staffs had occurred too hastily before the taking over of certain functions by volunteers had been properly prepared and organized (also the wages of paid functionaries of the lowest rung were unjustifiably low), while at the same time territorial-administrative units were sometimes excessively enlarged, which meant a separation of the Soviets from the people.

While most of these matters had already been corrected, the group's investigations in Kazakhstan had disclosed certain other problems.

The author noted that Lenin's original formulation that "all power, centrally and locally, belongs to the Soviets," has been retained in successive Constitutions. Thus, they write, while other organizations of Soviet society have their own specific fields of activity and work in cooperation with the Soviets, "the power of the state in the USSR is personified by the Soviets and effectuated through them. Only the Soviets have the right and duty to embody full state power, to issue decisions binding upon all and to supervise their execution. Only the Soviets and their agencies possess the authority characteristic of government and can, when necessary, apply compulsion through power of the state. This holds for the entire system of Soviets, both central and local." While the Communist Party has the role of political leader, it "by no means supplants the Soviets or other organizations."

The authors say that too often present day writers on the Soviets and their functions create the impression "that the governmental aspect in the organization and functioning of the Soviets is something residual, secondary, and the quicker it withers away the better." And that they therefore concentrate on "demonstrating the absence of fundamental differences between the Soviets and volunteer organizations."

In their own investigation the authors found the concept of the Soviets as *solely* volunteer organizations quite widespread at the local

---

* See the article "Increasing the Role of the Soviets: An Immediate Task," by V. Chkhikvadze, I. Pavlov and I. Azovkin, *Sovety Deputatov Trudiashchikhsia*, 1965, No. 8. Translation published in *Soviet Sociology*, Spring, 1966, International Arts and Sciences Press.

Nina Morozova, elected deputy to the Supreme Soviet at age 25. She was elected team leader of this Communist Labor Brigade at the Kuibyshev electrical works.

level, leading in some cases to violation of the proper relationships between government and volunteer organizations.

They said that for example there were numerous cases in the Kazakh Republic of violations of legislation pertaining to collective farms yet not a single case had been found where the rural Soviet had intervened. The Soviet authorities gave as the reason that, since the collective farms were voluntary organizations, the Soviet had no right to intervene. Cases had also been found where both the Komsomol and the Trade Union Regional Council had duplicated many matters that fell within the jurisdiction of the Soviets alone, and had gone so far as issuing instructions to the Soviets on such matters.

The authors cited instances of various Party organizations supplanting the Soviets and their machinery, deciding many questions within the province of the Soviets, regulating the work of the local Soviets in detail, and issuing instructions to personnel of the Soviets over the heads of the *Ispolkoms.* Another practice was the issuance of joint decisions by Party Committees and the Executive Committees of local Soviets on which only the latter really had the right to act.

An instance was cited in which the District *Ispolkom,* acting on telephone instructions from Party agencies, had assigned 78 hectares of land planted to cotton by the Lenin Collective Farm to the Chimkent Tire Works. When the collective farmers objected, the regional agencies insisted that the land had to be taken because drawings for the building of the plant on this land had already been made, "before the agreement of the collective farm had been obtained," add the authors indignantly. This was cited as a case where "the local government agency had not been bold enough to resolve on its own a problem directly within its jurisdiction." The authors felt the Soviets should in general make fuller use of their supervisory powers in the field of land condemnation and utilization.

Another thing the group found was that while housing, schools. stores, hospitals, consumer services and cultural institutions are supposed to function under the direct guidance of the local Soviets, the actual process of transferring them has gone very slowly.

The authors pointed out that this interfered with "a unified urban development policy," and complicated services to the population. They held that the concentration of housing, consumer and socio-cultural services into a single set of hands, which is now supposed to be done, is "advantageous both to the people and the state."

Sociological Studies of Deputies' Work

IT IS interesting to note that in the case of the work of the Soviets, as now in all areas of Soviet society, it is no longer considered sufficient to issue decrees as to how they shall operate, but detailed sociological studies are being made as to how the decrees are working out and what further changes need to be made. Questionnaires are sent out and polls taken on various aspects of the work, and computers are used to analyze the results.

One such investigation had to do with the amount of time deputies to local Soviets spent on their duties. It was carried on by personnel of the Law Sector of the Institute of Economics of the Estonian SSR, the Department of History of Tartu University, and the Computer Center of the University. It was described in an article by I. Kalits, A. A. Lamets and Kh. Kh. Shneider, "Use of the Method of Concrete Sociology to Study the Work of Deputies."*

Factors considered included the amount of time needed to perform duties, whether this coincided with working time and to what degree, whether the time expended on functions as a deputy was used ration-

---

* In *Sovietskoe Gosudarstvo i Pravo,* 1965, No. 9. Translation published in *Soviet Law and Government,* Winter 1965-66, International Arts and Sciences Press.

ally, how effective the deputy's activity was, whether it was affected by education, age, occupation, sex, party affiliation, etc., which factors promoted and which hindered the deputies' work, and how the training of deputies, exchange of experience etc. should be organized so as to take their own desires into consideration to a maximum degree. Altogether some 994 deputies to various types of local Soviets of Estonia were queried, about 8.5 per cent of the total number. The 27 questions fell into three groups: personal information, activities as deputies and proposals for improving the work of deputies.

The answers showed wide variation in the amount of time spent by deputies on their duties, with the largest number, 408, spending an average of only one to five hours monthly on their deputies' duties, 16 an average of over 40, and all manner of variations between. Least time was given by deputies from 25 to 29, explained by the fact that they are over-burdened with other civic duties, studying in higher educational institutions, etc. As age increases, the number of hours given to work as a deputy increases up to the age of sixty, then diminishes somewhat, although the older deputies get the more speeches they make!

The higher the educational level, the more time is spent by deputies on their work with the Soviet. More time is spent by department heads and others in executive positions, and by engineers, teachers, physicians and other professional people, than by production workers and collective farmers. In general city deputies spend more time on their work than those of rural Soviets. As a rule time given to deputies' work does not coincide with working time, but in a considerable number of cases it does.

Most of the deputies questioned gave, as the main difficulty encountered, lack of sufficient experience as deputies. A large number declared that they received little help from organizations supposed to aid them such as the Party, trade union, Komsomol, management at their place of employment, etc. The main types of aid required by deputies were listed as follows:

1) Regular seminars and conferences; 2) more literature on the work of the Soviets and the deputies; 3) establishment of the best possible material conditions for performance of the deputies duties; 4) more assistance from higher agencies and the provision of instruction in the localities; 5) greater attention to the proposals of the Soviets and deputies.

The authors, having established how unequally the burdens of office are borne by the deputies, concluded that one of the most important tasks is the establishment of conditions making it possible for all deputies to give maximum time to their duties, and the most rational utilization of their time. They also felt that their work demonstrated the great importance of sociological studies in all areas of the work of the Soviets and recommended great attention to the methodology of such studies in the future.

Chapter 5

OTHERS' IMPRESSIONS—NEW MEASURES

IT IS always salutary to check one's own impressions and factual material against those of others who are students in the same field. As I was writing this series, I came upon the April 1966 issue of *Soviet Studies,* a scholarly journal edited at the University of Glasgow, Scotland. It contained an article entitled "Soviet Local Government Today," by L. G. Churchward, Senior Lecturer of the Political Science Department of the University of Melbourne, Australia. It was based on his observations in the USSR in September 1964 (when I myself was there) and for three months in the winter and spring of 1965. As a guest of the Institute of State and Law, attached to the All-Union Academy of Sciences, he made a special study of local government. I found that the information he gathered was similar to that which I have presented, and it was particularly interesting to me to find that the conclusions of the author were very similar to my own.

An Australian Scholar's View

MR. CHURCHWARD made a strong point of the role of public organizations and volunteers in the work of the Soviets. He listed a whole series of "social organizations" in the RSFSR as of 1964. This listing throws light on an aspect of Soviet society little known to the outside world. It is usually considered that absolutely nothing happens in the Soviet Union that does not go through Government or Party machinery. These social organizations are, in a very real sense, volunteer organizations of the people, independent, but working closely with the local Soviets, usually in cooperation with the various Standing Commissions already described.

Herewith the list as given by Mr. Churchward: Street and House Committees; Parents Committees in schools, kindergartens, creches and apartment houses; Councils of medical institutions, Councils of clubs and libraries; Councils for assisting the improvement of living conditions; Women's Councils; Pensioners' Councils; Volunteer Fire Brigades; Volunteer Militia; Comradely Courts; Commissions on Control of Socialist Property; Technical-Production Councils in enterprises (or groups of enterprises), and in state and collective farms; Councils of kolkhoz brigades; Shop and Restaurant Commissions; Councils of Elders; Sanitary Posts and Brigades; Pensioners' Commis-

59

sions in establishments and enterprises; and a final listing, "other organizations." There were in 1964, in different parts of the RSFSR alone, 966,412 of these various organizations, with a total membership of 9,774,372 (there are probably many more today).

This list notes a number of public, or social, organizations that I had not heard about. There are also certain organizations belonging in this category which Mr. Churchward fails to mention, such as "Znanye" ("Knowledge"—formerly the "Society for the Dissemination of Political and Scientific Knowledge"), special Councils of Artists, Architects, Composers, etc., attached to many of the Soviets, Guardianship Councils and other new Councils and organizations constantly arising on the initiative of the people. Also working closely with the Soviets are such important organizations as the trade unions, the consumers' cooperatives and the numerous voluntary sport organizations one now finds everywhere.

Mr. Churchward found that in the regular departments of the Soviets the replacement of paid staff by non-paid, volunteer personnel had proceeded most rapidly in departments of trade, housing, municipal services, education, culture and organizational-instruction work (the latter has to do with mobilizing the forces for canvassing and instruction in any campaign in which the general population has to be involved).

He considered the "most impressive" developments in enhancing the role of the Standing Commissions of the local Soviets to be the trend toward transferring to them administrative rather than merely advisory functions. He notes that instances of complete liquidation of the Soviet Departments, their functions being transferred to the Standing Commissions, were found most often in fields of culture, trade, health and education. This tendency he finds to have progressed further in village, workers' settlement and rural district Soviets than in the large city Soviets.

Mr. Churchward made the point, with which I would certainly agree, that many of the social organizations noted function "spasmodically and ineffectively." I am sure their performance varies greatly from place to place, depending on local conditions, the type of leadership available and other factors. Nevertheless, the Australian professor finds that "on the other hand there can be little doubt that public participation in local administration has been steadily expanded over the past decade and that fundamental local matters such as housing allocation and maintenance, expansion of kindergarten and nurseries, allocation of places in boarding schools, health, trade and social services *are being increasingly controlled by these grass roots organizations*" (italics added).

The Australian educator further emphasized that while many of these democratic reforms were initiated in the regime of Khrushchev, there were also abuses of democracy under his leadership and that renewed emphasis on real collective leadership and on strengthening democratic forms of government accompanied Khrushchev's removal.

In describing elections, the author makes clear the very wide public participation in the nomination process. He speaks approvingly of the practice of candidates giving very full accounts of themselves at public meetings, and the requirement placed on party and government organs that they give a full report to the electorate on past accomplishments and future plans, with full allowance for criticisms, alteration and endorsement. While sometimes cut and dried, such meetings, he says, often give rise to very sharp criticisms on the part of the electorate and a "no-nonsense" voicing of demands. He also speaks of the hundreds of thousands of house-to-house canvassers who get the views directly of those voters who may not attend meetings.

Describing the election procedure, he says that only about one in fifty voters enters the screened off booth where he may delete the name of the candidate nominated, and that far from becoming a marked person in the community thereby, no one pays any attention at all.

While perhaps somewhat more restrained than my own conclusions, Mr. Churchward's should be recorded:

> Soviet local government is changing steadily. It is becoming less official and more "voluntary," more broadly based and less bureaucratic. If mass participation in the process of government is the key to democratic government, then local Soviets have progressed some way toward democratic government. Public participation is greater than it is in most other countries and it is increasingly effective at this local level. But the amount and success of public participation lessens in the higher levels of government. . . .

In the light of recent decisions of the Supreme Soviet, it is clear that the Soviet leaders are now seeking to increase public participation in the higher as well as the lower levels.

New Measures to Improve Work of Soviets

IN HIS SPEECH at the 23rd Congress of the Communist Party in June 1966, Nikolay Podgorny, President of the Presidium of the Supreme Soviet, stated frankly that the people do not yet fully utilize their Constitutional rights in relation to the Soviets, that the level of organizational work is often much too low and that the deputies themselves do not always show enough initiative. He declared that under the new five-year plan (1966-70) it is envisaged that the organs of state power and the largest mass organizations will exert a still greater influence than they have in the past on economic and cultural affairs.

Furthermore, he pointed out, along with the economic reform which puts greater responsibility on economic enterprises as such, greater emphasis than before is now to be placed on making sure that *all* problems of local importance are handed over to local organs for solution. Economic executives are enjoined to respect and adhere to the decisions of the local Soviets. This has not always been the case in the past. Since all but local industry is state controlled, state industries have to a large extent considered themselves independent and subordinate only to the regional *Sovnarkhoz* (Economic Council), during the period when these organizations existed, or to a branch of the corresponding industrial ministry of the republic or of the USSR. While this line of authority remains in force on production problems to a great extent, the work of the enterprises is now to be coordinated with local needs.

President Podgorny emphasized that while the Party organs must always be ready to give the local Soviets, city or village, whatever help or guidance they require, the Party must never under any circumstances take over any of the functions of the Soviets whatsoever, as has too often been done in the past.

Podgorny also laid stress on the very great importance of the village Soviets as the primary link in Soviet power. In the future it is envisaged that the rural Soviets are to play a greater role in the democratic guidance of collective farm life and also in helping to solve agricultural problems.

The role of these village Soviets, Podgorny continued, was more important than ever in these days when the villages were beginning in some respects to take on the aspects of the towns. These primary organizations, which are in direct contact with millions of working people, have the responsibility to render all-round assistance to the population in every aspect of life and to coordinate the work of all the agencies and enterprises, social, cultural, agricultural and industrial, under their jurisdiction. There had, he said, been great defects in the work of the local Soviets during the past five-year plan. In Azerbaidzhan, for example, while many new hospitals had been built in the countryside, the actual plan was only fulfilled by 46 per cent. The plan for building pre-school establishments in Kazakhstan had been fulfilled by only 67 per cent, and the plan for building schools in villages and collective farms in Turkmenistan, had been fulfilled by only 68 per cent.

Turning to the work of the Supreme Soviet, he said this leading organization of Soviet power must also play a greater role in the future. Already the people were making more demands on the deputies. Here he mentioned the recall of 350 deputies of all levels last year, ten of whom had been deputies of the Supreme Soviet.

Podgorny also stressed the necessity of raising the powers of the Procurator's office to insure that all legal requirements are met, and that the rights and interests of the working people are thereby protected against violations. There must be a more energetic struggle, he said, against all manifestations of bureaucracy on the part of any government organization, and against any indifferent or offhand attitude to proposals made by the working people.

More Standing Commissions for Supreme Soviet

THE 23rd CPSU CONGRESS, following Podgorny's report, decided on further steps toward implementing the decisions on extending the democratic functioning of the Soviets at all levels.

The meeting of the Supreme Soviet that followed in August 1966 adopted measures expanding its own democratic functioning, especially through the setting up of new Standing Commissions. These measures were outlined in a further report by Podgorny to a joint session of the Soviet of the Union and the Soviet of Nationalities.

He told the deputies that henceforth the Supreme Soviet would have to give more detailed attention than in the past to the problems of the economy and raising the living standards of the people, involving close study of all questions relating to the development of industry, agriculture, construction, public education, science, culture, public health, trade and social maintenance, and to the new legislation necessary in every field, as well as checking up on proper observance of existing legislation by bodies accountable to the Supreme Soviet.

Podgorny said that practice had shown that the work of the Standing Commissions is the major form of insuring participation by the deputies in decisions on all state matters and for insuring informed and comprehensive discussion at the Supreme Soviet sessions. The Standing Commissions act as auxiliary and preparatory bodies to both houses of the Soviet Parliament, discussing and analyzing in advance the questions to come before the sessions, introducing pertinent proposals and supervising the carrying out of Supreme Soviet decisions by executive agencies.

Hitherto, the two Houses have both had Standing Commissions only on the budget, on legislative proposals, on foreign affairs and on credentials, while the Soviet of Nationalities has had in addition an economic commission. Experience has shown that the budget commissions inevitably had to consider also the economic plans, which are always subject to endorsement by the Supreme Soviet as a whole, and that the whole range of subjects on which Standing Commissions are needed has widened. Podgorny proposed, and the deputies agreed, that in the future both the Soviet of the Union and the Soviet of Nationalities would have Standing Commissions on the following:

Planning and budget; industry, transport and communications; building and the building materials industry; agriculture; public health and social maintenance; public education, science and culture; trade and public services; legislative proposals; foreign affairs; credentials. Porgorny outlined their functions as follows:

They will consider the summary indices of the plan and budget, economic balance sheets, aspects of the proportionate development of the various branches of economy, links between them, etc. The commissions will analyze the revenue and expenditure sides of the state budget for the various branches of the economy and for the different Union Republics, as well as the federal budget, the Union Republic budgets, the rates of growth in the national income and the population's real income.

For the detailed study necessary in certain fields it has been necessary to form a number of sub-commissions in the Standing Commissions on economic and legislative questions. Standing Commissions analogous to those of the Supreme Soviet have been found essential in the Supreme Soviets of the Union Republics. The increased volume of work devolving upon the Standing Commissions has made it necessary to increase their numerical composition, to draw into the discussions deputies who are not members of the commissions, and to draw in many specialists and representatives of public organizations.

Mr. Podgorny said that while much had been accomplished by Standing Commissions in the past, there had been shortcomings in their work which must be corrected; discussions were often not sufficiently fundamental, participants not adequately informed.

In the future, he said, there must be more regular reports to the commissions by government ministries and departments, and more public discussion of matters under consideration would be held. Special requirements of the Union Republics and other national formations must be more fully taken into account. In the future the foreign relations commissions would give more extensive consideration to questions of economic, scientific, cultural and other contacts with other states and to the work of Soviet representatives in international organizations. Close collaboration between the different commissions on overlapping matters will be necessary, including joint sessions and joint sub-commissions. Greater coordination of the work of the Standing Commissions must be carried out by the Presidium, acting for the Supreme Soviet between sessions. More effective steps must be taken for relieving deputies of production or official duties when they are needed for commission work. Government officials will be required to submit needed materials and documents more promptly than in the past and vigorous measures must be taken "to stop such impermissible practices as when certain officials do not give timely replies to deputies' statements and requests and do not take measures on their proposals."

Podgorny said that the formation of the new Standing Commissions and improvement of their functioning would "make it possible to intensify in every way the activities of the Supreme Soviet, its Chambers and the Presidium, and help to develop further the principles of Soviet statehood. Favorable conditions are being created for a new upsurge in the activity of the deputies, which makes it possible to use to a greater extent the knowledge and experience of the deputies and to take into account the opinions of the electors."

Chapter 6

THE RURAL SOVIETS

THE organizational structure and the functions of the city Soviets and district Soviets within the cities, as described in previous articles, all apply to the rural Soviets. They also have their regular departments with whatever paid professional help is necessary to their functioning, and corresponding standing commissions through which the volunteer activity of the people of the countryside is enlisted and their direct participation in the work of government encouraged.

In the rural Soviets, as well as those of the cities, the deputies are required to have close ties with the population, take care of their needs and carry out their mandates.

The main differences between urban and rural Soviets are of course determined by the differences between city and countryside generally. Each will have departments corresponding to the needs of the people they serve. Many departments of city Soviets will be missing in village Soviets, and the latter as a rule will be mainly concerned with agricultural problems. Questions of education, culture, health and various community and social needs are also under the jurisdiction of the rural Soviets, but will sometimes be concentrated in the next stage above the village Soviet, the regional Soviet, covering a wider area.

In addition to many major matters, the village Soviets must take care of thousands of ordinary but very important and necessary affairs. They register births and build roads, provide transportation for emergency hospital cases, carry through village improvements and see to public order, take care of school repairs and insure that stores, canteens, and public baths function well. Their doors must be open from early morning until late at night, often the only time farmers can come. People come for advice, with requests, with legitimate complaints or just with a tale of woe to be shared. Someone must be there to listen, to do what has to be done.

THE greater differences in rural conditions in different areas than in city life mean that it is far more difficult to generalize about them. Some rural Soviets are coterminous with collective farms. This happens in cases where several villages have been completely collectivized and merged into one large collective farm.

In such cases, the activities of the Soviets coincide closely with those of the collective farm. In other cases, the village Soviet might comprise both collective and state farms, where the problem would be somewhat different because of the two different organizational forms. In still other areas there are local industries where some of the people might be working while others are engaged in agriculture, such different types of employment sometimes occurring within the same family. Or again, some villages are close enough to big cities for some of its residents to be employed in the city, or close to some industrial enterprises or new construction project providing employment. The rural Soviets thus sometimes have a very varied population to look after. While rural life is much less complex in many ways than that of the city, this by no means signifies that the work of the Soviets is simpler. Greater distances and a less concentrated population create special problems of transport and organization.

Within the responsibility of the rural Soviets falls the most basic problem of Soviet society. This is the problem of overcoming the age-old backwardness of the peasant, and of bridging the gap between town and country. This means great efforts to increase agricultural production through the application of the most modern scientific methods, with the farmer drawing closer to the skilled industrial worker, and raising individual productivity as well. And along with this, the raising of living standards and increasing the educational and cultural opportunities of village life to bring them close to those offered by the cities.

WHILE I visited a number of collective farms during my 1964 visit and learned something of the continuing problems of rural life and its tremendous advances since the twenties, when I first knew the Russian village, and since the days immediately following World War II, my stay was not long enough to permit any detailed study of how the rural Soviets operated. (This I hope to accomplish on another trip.)

In any case, 1964 would evidently have been a rather unpropitious time to observe the working of the Soviets in the countryside.

This, it will be remembered, was the summer prior to Khrushchev's removal, one of the main causes of which was an acute crisis in agricultural production. It was of course greatly to Khrushchev's credit that he insisted on bringing out into the open many problems concealed in the Stalin period, that he traveled widely, visiting farms and industries, talking to local people about their problems. But the trouble was that Khrushchev was not equipped to handle the vast problems with which he was faced, and failed to take advantage of the advice of trained specialists. He would become obsessed with some particular panacea, like the planting of corn, only to drop that for something else. He organized and reorganized, started a new scheme before a previous one demonstrated whether it was workable. One of his errors was the division of Party committees into two branches, one for industry and one for agriculture, which at the same time resulted in the division of the Soviets in the rural areas into an agricultural Soviet and an industrial Soviet. This caused the greatest confusion, since in so many districts there were both agricultural and industrial workers, who had the same kind of problems, used the same schools, hospitals, stores and other social and cultural institutions. The division into two separate Soviets, rather than following the logical method of having special departments for agriculture and for industry within the same Soviet, led at times to incredible waste and duplication. Constant handing down of new orders from above, since corrected, encouraged bureaucratic hangovers and stymied initiative.

Unified Party Committees and unified Soviets were restored shortly after Leonid Brezhnev became General Secretary of the Communist Party and Alexey Kosygin Chairman of the Council of Ministers. Agriculture received new attention. More rational forms of organization were introduced. More democracy was called for and instituted in the collective farm organization as well as in the Soviets, and far more local initiative provided for in the planning of production and organization and management of the work of both collective and state farms.

These measures resulted in the biggest harvest in history in the autumn of 1966. Good weather helped—but more important were the practical steps outlined and the raising of initiative through more democratic procedures.

IVAN GAVRILOV, a Novosti reporter, visited the town of Durykino about sixty miles north of Moscow, in the autumn of 1966, to observe how the village Soviet worked. This is the description he sent me:

"At the big building occupied by the *Ispolkom* [Executive Committee] of the Kirov Village Soviet, I was met by its chairman, Vassily Ulovkov. This Soviet, he told me, served the large village of Durykino and several small villages. About 7,000 people lived in this area, many of them employed in the state farm which is its leading enterprise, and the poultry factory. There were 60 deputies in the Soviet. All the deputies, with the exception of the Chairman and Secretary of the Soviet, were employed at regular jobs, giving their time to work as deputies without pay.

"Ulovkov took me around to meet some of the deputies. At the secondary school, teaching his physics class, I met deputy Sergey Yudin, principal of the school. He told me he had been working

67

at the school for sixteen years. As a deputy he had many duties in helping the people on many matters, but his main work was helping the Soviet carry out its education program, and enlisting parents to help in school problems. 'When I first came here,' he told me, 'there were only 249 children in school. Now we have 800. Our school, now in this well equipped, four-story, stone building, used to be in a primitive log building. There are also four elementary schools within the territory of our Soviet, which it has established and looks after.'

"Helena Ostrovskaya, a vigorous young woman who had just been elected to the Soviet for the first time, we found working in the village hothouse, where onions and cucumbers are grown. She immediately started talking to the Chairman about the necessity of extending the greenhouses.

"Next I met Deputy Nina Desvetova, an energetic young woman recently graduated from an agricultural school. Her specialty was cattle breeding. Ulovkov also introduced me to Deputy Anatoli Bobrov, head mechanic of the state farm, who was at work repairing a tractor. I met other deputies at their work in our rounds that day at the poultry farm, the hospital, and clinic, the large rural club with its fine auditorium for entertainment, lectures and movies, its library and rooms where amateur art groups were at work. In this way, by showing the deputies at their work, Ulovkov showed me in the most graphic way the closeness of the Soviet's ties with the people.

"Ulovkov told me that the Soviet also helps in the building of houses and in the over-all planning of further construction in the area and is responsible for protecting the natural resources of the territory —the pine and birch woods that surround it, the rivers and lakes. They have regular general meetings where the villagers come to discuss their needs, the cultural and public services to the population and village improvement generally.

"On matters of village improvement, the Soviet had repaired the roads connecting the villages in their area and built new ones, built seven large and 30 small bridges, built a dam, cleaned out several water reservoirs, and planted thousands of trees with the help of the population, for beautification purposes.

"I asked how the work of the Soviets was financed. The Chairman told me its budget was made up of deductions from the profits of the enterprises situated within its territory, from insurance collections, taxes and additional money which the local residents decide to contribute for special projects decided on at general meetings. When necessary, loans could be secured from the District Soviet, the next higher organ of state power.

"Ulovkov smiled when I asked whether it was possible to draw in many members of the population for volunteer work in the Soviet. All their work, he told me, was largely done with the help of volunteers, though he felt improvements could still be made in this.

Left: Machinist Anatoli Markov, elected to Orel City Soviet by fellow workers. Right: Varvara Koklyushkina, Chairman of the Liubertsy City Soviet, presiding at a meeting.

"I found that volunteer activity was organized through the following standing commissions: on agriculture, finance and budget, village improvement, trade and public services, health, law and public order, public education and culture. In addition 150 of the local residents are members of various public organizations which come under the supervision of the standing commissions. These include street and parents' committees, comradely courts, volunteer fire brigades, public councils of the clubs and libraries, a council of pensioners, a council for the protection of nature and so on."

AS THEY entered 1967, both the Soviet Government and the Communist Party determined on further measures for the improvement of agricultural production and life in the countryside. Early in March, the Central Committee of the CPSU and the USSR Council of Ministers, following a discussion in both bodies, issued a decision "On Improving the Work of Village and Township Soviets." Their special concern was drawing the people of the countryside into the work of administering state affairs on as extensive a level as is the practice in the city Soviets.

An article in *Pravda*, March 11, described this decision and also stressed its importance. It pointed out that village and township Soviets constitute the biggest link in the whole system of local Soviets.

There are about 40,000 such Soviets and almost 1,500,000 deputies, representing a population of 110,000,000 people, in a territory of 700,000 inhabited places, that include 36,000 collective farms and almost 12,000 state farms, as well as a wide network of industrial enterprises and a great variety of social, cultural and service institutions. These deputies, scattered over the whole countryside, must work in the very heart of the people, coming into daily contact with them on the most diverse matters.

The Party and Government decision noted that the local Soviets, who represent and carry out the authority of the state, must settle directly many questions relating to the daily needs of the people. It said that most deputies do their work conscientiously, carry out the mandates of their electors and report to them regularly, yet "the level of the work of many township and village Soviets lags behind life's demands," and that often they "do not fully utilize their rights or exert sufficient influence on the affairs of collective farms." As a result, there were still many shortcomings in the work of schools, hospitals, kindergartens and nurseries, stores, clubs and other organizations serving the people, for which the Soviets are responsible. In many cases organizational work of the Soviets fails to find practical solutions for problems of economic and cultural development. Burning questions of the life of the village and the township were not taken up often enough at the sessions of the Soviet or its *Ispolkom*. Meetings were too routine. Many Soviet officials lacked sufficient initiative in drawing public-spirited citizens, especially rural intellectuals, into volunteer work in the field for which they are best fitted.

It was not alone the local Soviets and their officials who were to blame for this, according to the decision. Party and Government bodies of the next higher rank did not give them the necessary help. It was necessary to provide special training facilities, short or even long term courses, for people who are drawn to work in the Soviets and have won the confidence of the people they represent.

All levels of the Communist Party organization were instructed to take all possible measures to liven up the work of the Soviets on economic problems of the collective and state farms, on local industry and trade, public catering and all kinds of public service establishments, and to make use of all local resources and potentialities to advance agricultural and industrial production and enhance the well-being of the people.

The decision at the same time contained an interesting warning: that there must in no event be any Party interference in economic and productive activities, and never any usurpation of powers. The role of the Party should only be one of stimulating, of helping, of making new resources available, of checking up when necessary on fulfillment of plans—but never, never to take over any of the functions of the Soviet. Rather they must help raise the role and the initiative of the deputies. Party members were particularly enjoined to heed criticism from the people.

If in the process of checking up deputies were found to be not properly fulfilling their duties and responsibilities, if the people complained that their needs and mandates were not being properly attended to, then measures must be taken to insure that the people know of their right to recall any deputy they feel to be derelict in his duty to them.

The decision stressed the necessity of observance of democratic principles in the activities of the collective farms as well as of the Soviets, of insuring proper use of the land, observance of Socialist legality, the protection of public order and of the rights of all citizens.

Above all, it dwelt on the necessity of evoking a conscientious attitude to labor, whether it be productive work, cultural work, or work as a Soviet deputy, and to work painstakingly and unendingly for the satisfaction of the demands of the people. This is the way the *Pravda* article puts it:

> Exercising the powers given them by law, the village and township Soviets must constantly devote themselves to improving education, health services, social maintenance, trade and public catering, and the work of public service establishments, to improving villages and townships, housing and road construction, coordinating to these ends the efforts of collective farms, state farms, enterprises and organizations on the territory under their jurisdiction. It is this that constitutes one of the most important ways in which village and township Soviets exert influence on the development of socialist production.

More help was asked of higher Government and Party organs in improving the work of the local Soviets, in guiding the economic and cultural life in villages and townships, and improving "the style and methods" of their activity. Work among the masses must be enhanced, Soviets must hold sessions on all burning questions and draw in the greatest possible number of people. The people themselves must be drawn into discussion and doing something about all major questions affecting their lives—and minor ones too.

The rights of village and township Soviets in deciding local matters are to be enhanced. Salaries of those elective officials who are paid, to be raised.

Above all, democratic principles must be extended in the work of the Soviets, and their bonds with the people strengthened.

Let no one think a decision like this remains on paper. The instructions are widely publicized in newspapers, broadcast by radio and TV, carried to the smallest party committees and local Soviets in the farthest corner of the land. It will be made the heart of reports to the officials and to the people. Not all that it asks will be done everywhere, and nowhere perhaps all at once. But the sharper the criticism, the more they mean business. A revivifying of the local Soviets may be expected as one more important achievement of this first half century of socialism.

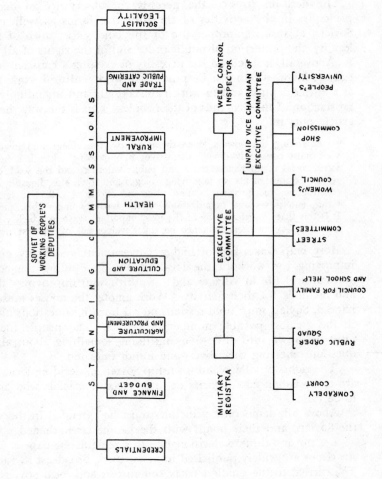

STRUCTURAL SET-UP OF NOVO-YEGORLYK VILLAGE SOVIET OF WORKING PEOPLE'S DEPUTIES IN SALSK DISTRICT, ROSTOV REGION

SOVIET OF WORKING PEOPLE'S DEPUTIES

STANDING COMMISSIONS

CREDENTIALS

FINANCE AND BUDGET

AGRICULTURE AND PROCUREMENT

CULTURE AND EDUCATION

HEALTH

RURAL IMPROVEMENT

TRADE AND PUBLIC CATERING

SOCIALIST LEGALITY

MILITARY REGISTRA

EXECUTIVE COMMITTEE

WEED CONTROL INSPECTOR

UNPAID VICE CHAIRMAN OF EXECUTIVE COMMITTEE

COMRADELY COURT

PUBLIC ORDER SQUAD

COUNCIL FOR FAMILY AND SCHOOL HELP

STREET COMMITTEES

WOMEN'S COUNCIL

SHOP COMMISSION

PEOPLE'S UNIVERSITY

Chapter 7

NEW DATA ON THE RURAL SOVIETS

ON MY latest trip to the Soviet Union, during July and August 1967, I visited Leningrad, Moscow, Baku, Tashkent, Samarkand, and in Siberia the Science City at Novosibirsk, Irkutsk, Bratsk and Lake Baikal. Among many vivid impressions of life in the USSR in its fiftieth anniversary year, I found the trend toward greater democracy and especially greater participation of the people in the process of government and self-government everywhere increasing and quickening. Progress in this direction was particularly emphasized in the preparations for the Fiftieth Anniversary celebrations. I found that the number of volunteers working in the Soviets' Standing Commissions had now increased to 25,000,000, two million more than on my previous visit.

I was unfortunately unable to carry out my desire to gather first hand material on the rural Soviets. I had a very full program and the time and the place I had set aside for visits to rural Soviets and talks with their deputies turned out to be at the very height of the harvest season when everyone was out in the fields, the most difficult time of all the year to get in touch with anyone having anything to do with agriculture and the least likely time for sessions of the Soviet to take place.

However, for the past year (1967-68) we have been receiving in our office the monthly magazine (in Russian) *Soviets of Working People's Deputies,* a manual designed to help Soviet officials and Soviet deputies in their work, which serves as an instruction book, a guide, a center for exchange of experiences and opinions. The magazine discusses everything, good and bad, that happens in the Soviets. In May 1967, the magazine started a "Correspondence Seminar for Workers of Village Soviets," for newly elected deputies or *Ispolkom* members.

The opening article of this department, on "Organs of State Power in the Village" (May 1967), stresses measures taken in recent years placing greater responsibilities on rural Soviets and calling for greater initiative on their part in planning, financial and agricultural questions, and the direction of local industry, as well as in social, cultural and domestic services to the population. The influence of the economic reform in fostering local initiative is being extended to the local

Soviets. It is made clear that local Soviets must break away from any subservience to higher government organs in the very clearly defined matters within their own competence; and there is renewed emphasis that the kind of Party tutelage that was often the case in the past must never be permitted, nor the usurpation by the Party of functions within the province of the Soviets.

By the same token, the Soviets themselves, while enjoined to play a more active role in helping improve agricultural production of the collective and state farms they encompass, are warned against interference with their affairs or the kind of supervision that is only within the competence of the agricultural departments (local branches of Ministry of Agriculture). No longer can there be any question of production goals being arbitrarily imposed from above, with quotas based on overall acreage rather than actual sowing capacity and crop yields. Collective and state farms take a direct part in drawing up plans on the basis of actual productive possibilities.

However, the article pointed out, there are many ways the Soviets can give practical help in the prompt fulfillment of plans, in providing needed transportation and supplies, keeping roads in order, and finding extra hands for seasonal work. (Young people often spend a

Latvian deputies to the Council of Nationalities, USSR Supreme Soviet, at the December 1968 session in Moscow. Left to right: L. F. Brangal, collective farm milkmaid; M. R. Gahlit, state farm calf tender; E. I. Yevdokima, plasterer; L. E. Zhukure, state farm milkmaid. Red Star order denotes Hero of Labor.

certain amount of vacation time on collective or state farms. A few years ago I visited the University of Irkutsk when the fall term had already started, to find the classrooms and dormitories all quite empty. The entire student body had answered an emergency call to help the *kolkhozes* in the neighboring countryside harvest their potatoes in the face of threatening rains.)

No aspect of village life from the cradle to the grave, according to the article, is outside the sphere of the rural Soviet's concern. It not only registers births, marriages and deaths, but helps arrange wedding celebrations or funerals if required. It is responsible for the management and activities of clubs, sanitary conditions and medical institutions, schools and libraries under its jurisdiction, and keeps an eye on institutions of this kind belonging to collective or state farms, although offering them assistance and recommendations rather than obligatory instructions.

The Soviet is responsible for the maintenance of law and order, carrying out preventive measures and working with local militia to apprehend law breakers. It is responsible for the Comradely Courts in the collectives or other institutions, in apartment houses or directly under the *Ispolkom*, and for the *druzhini* (Volunteer Public Order Squads). While in no way replacing courts, the Soviets have certain administrative rights and within limits can impose fines for damage to property of collective or state farms or other institutions by privately owned cattle or fowl, in cases of illegal home brewing of alcohol and so on.

The economic reform has its reflection in enhancing the responsibility of the Soviets in finding new budget resources and in helping both state farms and local industries to function profitably, which adds to the Soviet's income as well. Gone are the days when special projects initiated by the Soviets must depend on government subsidies, although such help is forthcoming in case of particularly difficult local conditions or natural disasters.

The *Ispolkom* (Executive Committee) of the Soviet has the responsibility for the day-by-day carrying out of decisions of the Soviets. But it is sharply stressed that all the most burning local questions, everything that affects the local population, its desires and needs, must come before the regular Soviet sessions for full and free exchange of opinions.

All deputies are required to report both to the Soviets and to general meetings of the electors. The article stresses the need of wide publicity for all the activities of the Soviet and full public information on how the mandates of the people are carried out. Public meetings of the Soviets should draw large attendance. Questions to be discussed must be posted in public places, in clubs, libraries, cinema halls, post office branches and so on, as well as in places of work.

The agenda must not be confined to long reports by the chairman and other officials. Reports must be brief, heads of various departments and commissions should report on their own work, and plenty of time be allowed for ordinary citizens to participate in general discussion.

There is repeated emphasis on the fact that the deputy is the central figure in the village Soviet, regularly participating in sessions and in the standing commissions. He must work in the very heart of the people, representing their interests, learning the needs and problems of each individual, keeping them abreast of every Soviet decision.

There is a reminder that when the village deputies do not keep close touch, when they fail to justify the confidence the voters have placed in them by electing them, or if they act in a way unworthy of their high calling, they may be recalled at any time. (Recall procedure described on page 00.)

The article concludes that despite considerable improvement of the work of rural Soviets in recent years, many weaknesses remain. Too often they neglect the practical needs of the collective and state farms, close their eyes to arbitrary use of collective land by other local or state institutions, ignore cases of high-handed, undemocratic management and bureaucracy, permit the erosion of citizen's rights and fail to provide essential communal improvements.

Part of the reason for this is attributed to lack of training and experience of newly elected deputies. To remedy this, courses have been established throughout the country for rural Soviet deputies. These last for three or four weeks, during which the deputies are given paid leave of absence from their regular jobs, and additional stipends for living expenses when necessary. Courses for the newly elected and less experienced may be longer. Lectures and seminars are given by experienced officials of higher organs. There are also brief refresher courses to keep deputies who have served longer periods abreast of modern methods.

The introductory courses cover a study of the role of the Soviets in the life of society, scientific methods of administration, improvement in style and methods of work and in forms of extending participation of all the people.

New textbooks and materials for these courses have been prepared.

Another method for improving the work of the rural Soviets is regular conferences of deputies and officials from different areas for the exchange and generalizing of experience.

Among the reasons given for the shortcomings of the rural Soviets is over-loading of the officials with too much paper work. Ordinarily, the only paid officials are the *Ispolkom* chairman and secretary, often only the latter, while the bulk of the work is carried on by non-paid officials, deputies and volunteers. This is considered all to the good.

The problem, however, according to complaints written in to the magazine by the secretaries themselves, is that they are given too many functions and too little technical help. The secretaries have to fill out all kinds of documents by hand since proper forms are not provided. Efforts are now being made to overcome this problem.

Standing Commissions of Rural Soviets

ANOTHER section of the "Correspondence Seminar" department deals especially with the work of the standing commissions of the rural Soviets. The report on this is written by V. Bocherov, Secretary of the Executive Committee of the Regional Soviet of Stavropol.

All deputies to the rural Soviets, as in the cities, participate in the standing commissions. In addition there are tens of thousands of "activists," that is, members of the population who regularly participate as volunteers in the work of the rural Soviets.

Members of the commissions are elected at the first session of newly elected rural Soviets for a period of two years. The number of members and the composition of the commissions varies from place to place. Most of the village Soviets in Stavropol Region, the author reports, have the following commissions: mandate; agricultural; budget-finance; culture, education and health; town improvement and roads; trade, communal and every day services; socialist legality and maintenance of public order.

Procedures on elections of standing commission officers are the same in rural and urban Soviets, with all officers sometimes elected by the standing commission, or in some cases the main officers being elected by a Soviet session.

Bocharov declared that the success of the standing commissions' activities depends on their having appropriate leadership. He cited as an example the case of the standing commission on education of the Velichayevsky Soviet, Levokumsky District, which after an initial spurt, came to a dead stop. The reason was that no one elected to the commission except the chairman, a bookkeeper, had any experience at all in the field of education.

Another example was Uroshinensky Soviet, where the chairman elected to head the village improvement and roads standing commission was the state farm agronomist. He was excellently qualified professionally for the job, but his own work prevented him from coming to the village except on rare occasions, so the activities of that commission were stalled for lack of guidance.

On the other hand, the Bezopasnensky Soviet in Izobilnensky District had elected to its standing agricultural commission: two agronomists, two *kolkhoz* brigade leaders, one link leader, one dairy farm director, three tractor drivers, two rank-and-file *kolkhoz* members. Every branch of agricultural work in the area was thus repesented and the commission worked very effectively.

As in the city Soviets, standing commissions, in addition to initiating activity and new projects, have the responsibility of checking up on and helping the activities of all organizations on the territory within their Soviet's jurisdiction. They can require any information desired and reports from people responsible. It is their duty to look into fulfillment of voters' mandates and complaints of citizens. Their instructions are mandatory for institutions that come under the budget and competence of the rural Soviet. In other cases they can only make recommendations.

The rights of standing commissions have been extended to certain executive functions. For example, the budget-finance standing commission may authorize the budget for a Soviet organization, distribute funds from the budgetary surplus, give loans to individuals for building homes or acquiring cattle for personal use, act on certain types of tax complaints, and so on. The standing commission on culture and problems of daily life may approve plans for village clubs, libraries, and other facilities, provide funds for school lunches, make decisions on placement of children in day nurseries and kindergartens, on distribution of goods to stores, on building materials, etc.

Standing commissions usually work on a three-month plan, within an overall plan of one or two years. Bocharov warns against cut-and-dried plans consisting mainly of such items as "To hear report of town improvement commission," and the like. This, he says, is not a plan. The work of standing commissions must include practical organizational work in the field.

On the question of coordinating activities with neighboring Soviets, Bocharov described a successful plan initiated by the standing commission on village improvement and roads of the Kursavsky Soviet, where several villages combined on a two-year program of roadbuilding and repair, bridge building, water supply system and the like. Every standing commission member was made responsible for some phase of the work, such as finance, transport, building materials or mobilizing large numbers for *voskresniks* (volunteer work on Sundays and other free time).

Bocharov recommended that sessions of the Soviet be held every month or so except in spring sowing and harvesting periods. Meetings must always be scheduled for non-working time; in any case, there must always be a quorum, with more than half the members present. Members not able to attend should be asked their opinion by phone on special questions to be discussed and all members must be promptly informed of decisions taken, with wide publicity among the general public as well. Careful, concrete preparations are required, and members of standing commissions are required to take an active part in the preparations.

Here is an example. Neither the rural Soviet nor any of its commissions has the right to give direct instructions regarding the internal organization in a collective farm. One of the members of the standing commission of agriculture of the Alexandrisky village Soviet, however, requested that the commission check up on the dairy farm of the local collective farm, where too many calves were being lost. Members of the standing commission inspected the dairy farm and found that unsanitary conditions and lack of proper care were the cause of the deaths of the calves, and drew up a list of recommendations which they presented both to the head of the dairy farm and the administration of the *kolkhoz*. Going back later to check up, they found that nothing had been done. The chairman of the standing commission then took up the matter with the *Ispolkom* which called in the collective farm management for impartial discussions. As a result, the *Ispolkom* decided to recommend that the head of the dairy farm be released as unfit for his duties. The collective farm management, after a general membership meeting of the *kolkhoz*, agreed on this step. The dairy farm was then put in the hands of an experienced veterinarian. The place was cleaned up, and a lying-in department for calving mothers and a prophylactorium were set up.

This cooperation was so successful that the *kolkhoz* on its own initiative asked the help of the standing commission in instituting a whole series of improvements in its orchards and gardens, extending electrification, installing telephones, carrying out a "sanitary" day once a month, and so on. After this successful experience with one *kolkhoz*, all the other *kolkhozes* in the area began to come to the standing commission for help.

On Organizing the Work of Rural Soviets

IGNATOV, *Ispolkom* chairman of the Annensky Village Soviet of Katalinsky District, Cheliabinsk region, answers a newly elected deputy's question about how the rural Soviet's work should be organized in the May 1967 issue of the magazine, by describing the work of his own Soviet as follows:

The Annensky Soviet covers an area with 5,000 inhabitants, concentrated in six communities. The majority are workers in grain state farms. There are also geological prospectors, lumber workers and personnel of children's sanitaria, a Young Pioneer Camp and various village institutions. In the area are 14 stores, four restaurants, several primary and intermediate schools, a House of Culture, three clubs, four libraries, several hospital annexes and medical centers, kindergartens and crèches. Eighteen different enterprises are directly on the budget of the Annensky Soviet.

Only the President and Secretary are full-time paid workers of the *Ispolkom*. The deputy chairman and six *Ispolkom* members have other regular jobs. Responsibilities are divided among them according to specialty, experience, organizing ability and free time.

The Soviet has five standing commissions headed by deputies, with 40 to 50 activists in each, and in addition 17 section committees of the Soviet, on a geographical basis.

The village improvement and roads commission, on which the lumber camp director was the leading spirit, was especially successful in getting out practically the whole population for *voskresniks*. Activists were divided into groups. Some planted, some built bridges, some were in charge of beautifying parks and squares. Four thousand trees and bushes were planted, over 5,000 flowering plants. A competition was organized for the most attractive and cleanest streets and houses. Forty citizens were awarded badges of honor.

The standing commission on trade worked very effectively. There had been complaints about poor service. The salespeople worked at their own convenience. Too often housewives found the door locked and could not buy food for supper or other needed supplies. Finally the commission was able to get *Centrosoyuz* (the consumer's cooperative organization) to institute a shift system and additional shop branches were established in more accessible locations.

The cooperatives were completely unprepared to meet the growing demand for refrigerators, washing machines, vacuum cleaners, accordions, guitars and other musical instruments. On the deputies' insistence the stores finally stocked enough of these things. Then it was found that the local machine and tractor station had failed to set up a repair shop, and soon all the housewives were screaming that their equipment was out of order. This also was rectified by the standing commission.

The standing commission on education made a valuable contribution in arranging for the transfer of village children from cramped, inadequate quarters to a large new school. Because of distances in the area it was necessary to make boarding arrangements for some of the older pupils. Kovrigina, herself a teacher, chairman of the commission, got busy and saw that the arrangements were made through the regional consumers' cooperative society for bed linen and meals, which the District Department of Education had failed to provide.

The standing commission arranged for the additional space necessary to solve the question of supervision of children of working families after school hours and on holidays.

The commission also cooperates closely with the parents' committees organized at every school, kindergarten and crèche. It helped set up a special summer camp for children whose parents had to work all day in the fields. It assisted in repairs of school buildings, in the equipment of school workshops and experimental fields, to carry out the polytechnical principle in education that all children shall become acquainted with the basic processes underlying agricultural and industrial labor.

Also helpful in the commission's work is the Women's Council, set up under the supervision of the Soviet although not technically a part of it. (Such councils are found all over the Soviet Union. This is an independent, people's organization working closely with the Soviets.) The Council organizes lectures for fathers and mothers and young people on medical and pedagogical themes. It gives consultations for housewives on more tasty cooking, on making comfortable and attractive clothes for children. The Women's Council carries on propaganda to instil love of order and beauty and it is largely the result of their work that one sees such an abundance of flowers around every home and institution in our area.

The standing commission on education and culture also works with the special councils of village cultural organizations. The clubs and libraries frequently hold readers' conferences, discussions, question and answer sessions, "meetings with well-known people." Concerts and performances are put on by our many amateur art circles. The commission, when desired, arranges marriage celebrations like those in the Palaces of Weddings in the cities. The serious ceremonial part is combined with the traditional village celebrations the people love—troikas driving through the streets with sleigh bells ringing in the winter, or flower-bedecked and beribboned carriages in the summer. There is plenty of the old time feasting and dancing—but, Ignatov assured his readers, they avoided their prolongation into several days of drinking bouts by some of the guests as was apt to happen in the past.

The standing commission on agriculture was especially effective. At least half the deputies drive tractors and combines or operate other types of machinery; or they are specialists in livestock raising, dairy farming, or some other branch. They help the *sovkhoz* make the best use of its land, utilize the latest scientific farming methods and technology and fight pests and weeds. The members of the standing commission work in close contact with the trade union of agriculture workers, check on the quality of repairs, on the care of machinery, on the condition of the fields in preparation for the spring sowing. Sometimes the machinery is not in good condition in the spring when it is most needed. What is most important is to be sure all repair work is completed during the winter months, in good time for plowing and sowing. The Soviet also helped provide 120 extra workers at harvest time, and assisted in insuring good living and working conditions for them.

The commission on socialist legality and public order works with five different comradely courts in the area, which handle petty crimes and prevent bigger ones, and cooperates with dozens of the volunteer people's militia, the *druzhini,* who help keep public order and guard the people's property and "combat uncultured manifestations" (by this is meant what the Soviets call hooliganism, usually the result of too much vodka, creating disturbances in public places, and just plain acting rude.) In the growing season, the *druzhini* patrol the fields and orchards and vegetable plots, guarding them against theft.

The Annensky Soviet had established throughout its territory a system of combined home service shops, where people can have all their needs attended to—a tailor and dressmaking establishment, which mends and makes over as well as making new suits and dresses; a shoe repair shop; a barber and hairdressing establishment, a section for general household repairs and help. Where distances are great, there are branches of these service centers within easy reach of the householders. They are even beginning to establish laundry and dry cleaning services, formerly unheard of in village areas.

Although they have accomplished a great deal, chairman Ignatov says he is far from satisfied with the work. There must be constant prodding to develop the initiative of the deputies and the people. Nothing can remain just on paper. "I, myself, as chairman," he writes, "feel I have to check up personally on all the most important decisions. I have to keep looking around, to see what's been done, what still remains to be done, talk to the people, to make sure all their needs are discussed at meetings and followed up. We must demand exactingness in ourselves and others, seek out new reserves both in people and in our resources, and always at all times draw the local population into our work and serve their needs."

Failures Faced Frankly

THUMBING through this magazine, one gets an extraordinarily frank picture of the problems, difficulties and shortcomings of the local Soviets as well as their achievements. Even the most successful acknowledge frankly the areas where they have failed.

The issue for August 1967, has an article entitled "Obstacles on Our Path" by I. Zukhov, chairman of the Deputies' Group of Moisseyev village, Tambov Region. Moisseyev, with over 400 households, is one of the eight population points of the Podgorny village Soviet. The deputies' group of twelve represents the Podgorny *Selsoviet*.

This group had difficulty establishing its authority. The author complains that while it had accomplished quite a lot, local and higher organizations often failed to take their proposals seriously.

"Perhaps not all of our proposals were useful," Zukhov wrote, "but still there should have been a more respectful attitude toward our requests and suggestions. As a pensioner I am able to give full time to my work as chairman, and it is my job to apply to government organizations on various matters. For example, the villagers wanted the Moscow-Kamyshev train to stop at the Moisseyev siding, only three kilometers away, as it used to do. Now that the trains do not stop there, the nearest railroad station is over twelve kilometers away, and you have to transfer, and there is a three hour wait.

"I wrote many appeals on behalf of the villagers about this to

All deputies are required to keep regular visiting hours for constituents. Supreme Soviet deputy Fyodor Tsanko talks over some personal problems with pensioners Paval Donch and Dmitri Zozulya at his office back home.

the Ministry of Transportation. The Regional Soviet *Ispolkom* supported me. But the Ministry paid no attention. They wrote that everything was satisfactory as it was. Correspondence dragged on for several years, and that meant that the people in Moisseyev, and in other nearby villages who were also concerned, gradually lost confidence in the ability of our deputies' group to accomplish anything. Finally some of our citizens started writing letters to *Izvestia*, and only after this public criticism did the Ministry finally take action and arrange for trains to stop at Moisseyev. We feel that the Ministry, as an organ of the government, should have acted at once on the appeals of the deputies' group, the local representatives of government, instead of ignoring them. How can the people be expected to uphold the authority of local government if higher government organs show no respect for it?

"Another example. A super-phosphate factory got permission to build a drainage canal right through the Lenin *kolkhoz* pasture. This was done without even notifying the *kolkhoz* management. There was no bridge, and the *kolkhoz* cattle were cut off from the best pasture land. The *kolkhoz* chairman himself finally got agreement from the factory to build a bridge, but nothing happened. The next spring our deputies' group asked the chairman of the district Soviet *Ispolkom* to take care of it. The factory director again promised to build the bridge. But the factory administration forgot all about the promise, and the District *Ispolkom* failed in its responsibility to insist on it.

83

It took a whole year before our deputies' group finally got the factory to build bridges over the canal and pay the *kolkhoz* for the use of its land.

"Of course we understand that the deputies cannot expect to walk along a smooth road and settle everything with the flourish of a pen," he concluded, "but it is necessary that they be listened to, that their authority should be upheld by other government agencies, and then so much time will not be wasted."

Chairman Sergeyev of the Karabikhsky village Soviet of Yaroslav Region writes (May 1967) that after a critical review of their work, they concluded that while they had big plans, too much remained unfulfilled. The Soviet and its *Ispolkom* expended their strength too often on minutiae, rarely consulted the voters, and relied too much on formal reports at Soviet sessions. So they set about improving things.

The sixteen cooperative stores in their area had been giving poor service. The Standing Commission on Trade, which had not been checking up on their work, organized a thorough investigation of all the stores to find out what was wrong. They studied the complaint books each store is required to keep and turned up such facts as cheating of customers by short weighting on scales adjusted for this purpose and overcharging laid to "lost" price tags. They found several stores with cramped premises where disorder reigned, goods were heaped up on counters, essential stocks lacking for want of storage space. Armed with the facts and complaints of customers, the standing commission invited all the store managers to a conference. They decided on what improvements could be made through their own efforts, and what help was required from the Soviet. Decided improvements are already under way.

A. Konev, of Krasnodar, writes (May 1967) that in the Kuban Region (North Caucasus) there are 358 village Soviets. Of these, 200 have a radius of five to fifteen kilometers. This is a manageable area, with no distances from the center being too great. But there are 116 village Soviets with a radius of fifteen to thirty kilometers, and the remaining 42 have a radius of over 30 kilometers, meaning that a large part of the population is too far from the center and the work of the rural Soviets becomes very complicated. He recommended a territorial reorganization to correct this situation.

Closing the Gap Between City and Country

S. ANDRIANOV, Assistant Chairman of the Council of Ministers of the Ukraine, and chairman of State Construction of the Ukrainian Republic, wrote in *Soviets of Working People's Deputies* for December 1967 of the special role of the Soviets in village construction work. This is part of the basic program of the Soviet Party and Government for closing the gap between city and country, and bringing more of the conveniences and amenities and cultural facilities of the cities to the rural population.

The Soviets are now being given the main role in carrying this out locally, helping to create their own economic base in collective and state farms and any local productive enterprises. The Soviets in the Ukraine are thus assigned a more responsible role than formerly in the rational planning and construction of the population centers, and the state is accordingly allocating more funds and bank credit facilities to them.

Andrianov said the amount of construction being done in the rural areas of the Ukrainian Republic during the jubilee year of 1967 included 538 new schools, 960 clubs and Houses of Culture, 1400 preschool institutions, 1,500 public baths, 300 restaurants, 100 home service and repair combinats, in addition to extensive building of new roads, new water and sewage systems, electrification lines and so on.

The Soviets, he said, were working with the district architects in coordinating the general construction plans for each given area. Standing commissions had also been drawn closely into this work, calling on all the local professional skill available, holding town meetings to report to the population and get their ideas. Andrianov stressed the necessity of submitting construction plans of collective and state farms to the rural Soviet to insure greater coordination and lack of duplication. Here an important consideration always had to be guarding against using for construction purposes, land best suited to agriculture through agreement between the enterprise in question and the Soviet.

Andrianov also spoke of the enormous amount of individual construction going on in the Ukrainian villages, amounting to about 100,000 new homes a year. Here too, he suggested that in so far as possible such building be brought into a general plan. Architects were helping with designs for attractive individual houses and projects for whole areas, where ancient houses were being replaced by more modern and convenient ones, with pleasing colors and designs.

He said it was important for the Soviet deputies to make surveys, find out where help was needed, who could build on their own funds, who needed loans, building materials, or other help. It was necessary to draw up preferential lists of those who were most needy or most deserving, such as invalids of war and labor, widows, single mothers, leading workers.

A number of collective and state farms had organized special building brigades to work for the members. He noted that more and more new dwellings in the countryside had inside plumbing.

While most of his report dealt with progress, he also spoke of instances of insufficient concern on the part of deputies, some limiting their acitivities to attending meetings—some not even doing that. Frequently the *Ispolkom* was at fault for depending too much on experienced workers and not involving others.

A STRIKING example of the constant concern of the Soviet Government with the expansion of the democratic rights and functioning of the people at the grass roots level has occurred as I have been completing these notes on the rural Soviets. This concern is demonstrated in a new decree of the Supreme Soviet of the USSR giving the rural Soviets new facilities to help solve some of the problems recorded in the preceding pages, and codifying measures proposed in recent years to improve the work of the Soviets into the law of the land.

From the reports of rural Soviet officials I have quoted, it appears that many of the local problems arise from jurisdictional complications, that is, the lack of authority of the local Soviets in relation to organizations and enterprises situated on their territory, but under the authority of some higher organ or government ministry. Other problems arise because of lack of financial or other needed resources.

All these problems and complaints have been studied by a special commission set up for the purpose. This commission gathered together all available material from the press and other sources and asked for further proposals from the governing bodies at all levels of all the Union Republics, ministries and government departments, research institutes, and from as many local Soviet workers who cared to express their opinions. On the basis of the commission's report and wide public discussion, the Presidium of the Supreme Soviet of the USSR, on April 8, 1963, issued a decree, enlarging on previous legislation, entitled "On the Fundamental Rights and Duties of the Village and Township Soviets of Working People's Deputies."

The decree is intended "to increase still more the role of the village and township Soviets of the Working People's Deputies in the solution of the problems of economic and socio-cultural development and of the improvement of the democratic principles of their activity."

The contents of the decree clearly reflect the process that has been taking place under the economic reform of 1967 whereby the initiative and responsibility of local enterprises are greatly extended. It spells out the fact that while the local Soviets are fully responsible, the various enterprises and organizations being directly subordinate to them, they also exercise control over the work "of the collective and state farms, enterprises of local industry, social services, trade and public catering, municipal economy, public health, education, communication and culture, situated on the territory of the Soviet and other organizations which may be subordinate to some higher body than the local Soviet but which directly service the population."

The rural Soviets, in the terms of the decree, are empowered to check on the observance of laws by such organizations, to hear reports of heads of enterprises and coordinate their activities in servicing the population. While the rural Soviet may not interfere in the internal affairs of such organizations as collective farms, consumers' cooperatives and other voluntary organizations of the people except in cases of law violation, its decisions and orders issued in conformity with its rights are obligatory.

Whereas formerly the rural Soviets had no authority in the drafting of economic and cultural construction plans, under the new decree they now participate in both annual and long-term plans of the collective and state farms and local industry, and also submit their proposals on housing, social and cultural services, amenities and trade. The decree gives to the local Soviets the right of coordinating and controlling all housing and other types of construction, all construction and repair of motor roads and provision of transport facilities for all disasters and emergencies.

The decree provides that the village or township Soviets have the final say regarding their own budget and its distribution and the right to allocate any additional resources acquired or remaining surplus. No higher body can withdraw any capital investments made by the village or township Soviet. Rural Soviets now not only control the collection of taxes but may grant reductions of local taxes and the agricultural tax in case of need, and may release low-income families from even the minimal payments for children's meals at school and for after-school care in the prolonged-day schools, arrange grants for individual housing construction and the like.

The village and township Soviets now have the right to decide on the allocation of additional plots of land needed for personal use of collective or state farm members or other workers in their area.

The decree recommends that higher government bodies insure that a substantial portion of funds appropriated for housing and welfare construction from proceeds of State industrial enterprises in the given area be put at the disposal of the village Soviet for the improvement of their communities, as well as insuring retention of revenues from services.

The village Soviets now have the right to approve the appointment of executives of schools, preschool institutions, extra-curricular establishments and public health and cultural institutions.

The decree provides that the term of office of the Chairman, Deputy Chairman Secretary of the Soviet Ispolkom is to be included in the work record of the basic profession of the incumbent of each of these offices. Also new stress is laid on insurance of release of deputies *with pay* from regular jobs during sessions of the Soviet.

The local Soviets now have full control of provision and distribution of housing facilities, fuel and light, both for the workers of its own enterprises and in endorsing housing plans of organizations not under its direct jurisdiction.

They are responsible for providing and repairing of premises for all social and cultural institutions and for general supervision over

87

work of schools and enforcement of general compulsory education.

A special provision enjoins the participation of rural Soviets, jointly with the trade unions, in the enforcement of labor legislation pertaining to labor protection in state and collective farms or industrial enterprises, in the observance of pension laws and other social security measures, in making special grants to those in need, such as those outside of pension coverage, single mothers with many children and citizens suffering as a result of natural disasters.

Within limitations providing that it can in no case substitute for the People's Court in matters solely under the latter's jurisdiction, the village or township Soviets may mete out administrative punishments in cases of violations of public order, of rules on maintenance of cleanliness in inhabited localities, of rules for protection of nature and cultural monuments, for abusing trade in alcoholic drinks, and for damaging crops in collective and state farms. For this purpose, a special administrative committee may be formed attached to the Soviet *Ispolkom* in cases of need and with permission of the superior Soviet's *Ispolkom*.

New Financial Assistance

IN FURTHER implementation of measures to enhance the rights and responsibilities of local Soviets, the USSR Council of Ministers passed a special resolution "On Measures for Enhancing the Material and Financial Basis of the Rural Soviets." This makes more explicit the measures indicated above for increasing revenues and for responsibility of rural Soviets for their use. In addition, the resolution provides for the construction or allocation for the work of all rural Soviets (in many cases still housed in dilapidated quarters) of adequate buildings, office equipment and transport.

David Frumhartz (standing) addresses a meeting of the trade union shop committee, to which the workers of the big Rostov farm machinery factory have elected him.

In the case of both the above-mentioned Supreme Soviet decree and this supplementary resolution, all-Union Republican Governments are asked to bring their own local legislation into conformity with them, with due consideration for special national and local conditions and needs.

The resolution calls upon the *USSR Gostroi* (State Construction Commission) to aid the rural Soviets by providing economically feasible standard designs for housing, both apartments and individual homes, and buildings for industrial, agricultural, social or cultural purposes, taking into account local conditions and available building materials. It also instructs all-Union and Autonomous Republics, territorial and regional government organs to provide for materials for rural construction needs in their economic development plans.

People's Control Bodies

NO DESCRIPTION of the operation of the Soviets at all levels could be complete without mention of the system of control bodies common to the Communist Party and the state, now called the Committee of People's Control of the USSR (formerly the Committee of Party and State Control). This is an organ set up jointly by the Central Committee of the Communist Party and the Council of Ministers and Presidium of the Supreme Soviet. The following description is taken in the main from "A Background to Political Democracy in the USSR," by G. Moiseyev and A. Ardatovsky. (Booklet published by Soviet Embassy, London, February 1965.)

These committees at all levels contain elected representatives (both Party and non-Party) of local Soviets, Party organizations, the Komsomol, the trade unions, the press, the workers, peasants and intellectuals. The basic working staff of the control bodies consists of volunteers from all sections of the population. At factories and other industrial enterprises, construction sites, collective and state farms, volunteers are elected at meetings of the working people to help the control committees. Each group contains from 15 to 35 members, with whatever sub-groups are necessary.

The main job of this control system is to check on the way Party and Government decisions are carried out, to eliminate shortcomings and to protect the interests of the people. The central groups are called upon to be especially alert in checking up on the way in which local Soviets are extending their democratic functioning.

The control teams have the task of helping to improve all branches of the economy and cultural and social life and to prevent any violations of the law or abuses of authority. To publicize their work, they are given full access to all information media such as the press, radio, films and TV, and are required to report regularly on their work to general meetings of the people, meetings of the Soviets and meetings of institutions with which they are connected.

They carry out their work mainly by persuasion, and by social censure of people found by their investigation to be lax in the enforcement of state discipline, and who are responsible for inefficiency and wastefulness.

More details were given on their work in an interview published by Novosti Press Agency on January 31, 1968, the 50th anniversary of the setting up of these control bodies. The interview, by correspondent Yevgeni Ivanov, was with Pavel Kovanov, Chairman of the USSR People's Control Committee, who provided the following facts.

The control organization was first set up by a decree of Lenin, who described its purpose as that of drawing in broad sections of non-Party people to check on all state affairs and to learn the business of governing themselves, to help perfect the government apparatus, eradicate bureaucracy, insure strict observance of legality and carry out the will of the people.

The control bodies have gone through various changes in connection with the needs of the time. Their role was seriously distorted during the Stalin era, but they have since been reactivated in connection with the greater stress on extending Soviet democracy.

Today there are more than 7,000 people on the staff of the People's Control bodies throughout the country. And over seven million volunteers carry on the work of the 900,000 control groups at various enterprises.

With the introduction of the new economic reform, the role of the people's controllers in the national economy has increased substantially. In implementing the government directives for more efficient management, people's control bodies have, in the last two years, for example, achieved a saving of more than 20 million kwh of electricity and more than 15 million tons of fuel. Their checkups have resulted in improving the work of trade and catering establishments, medical supplies, the work of hospitals, schools, children's establishments and homes for the aged and invalids.

Attention is called to the fact that the activities of the people's controllers go all the way to the top. They inspect the work of Government Ministries as well as local enterprises. Thus not long ago the Ministry of Machine-Tool and Instrument-Making Industry and the Ministry of the Electrotechnical Industry took measures to improve the quality of machine-tools and automatic transfer machines which the people's controllers had found not up to the highest standards.

It should also be understood that the task of the people's controllers is not only to ferret out and expose shortcomings, but also to propose more efficient methods, to help put into operation valuable proposals made by workers and promote scientific organization of labor. They organize competitions and reviews for this purpose, and utilize the regular production conferences of trade union workers and management.

In conclusion, Mr. Kovanov cited a recent instance at the Rostov Farm Machinery Plant. On the initiative of the People's Control group of the plant, a public review of better managerial methods was held, with the support of both trade union and management, in the course of which more than 10,000 proposals were made by the plant's workers. As a result 444 people were dropped by the administrative-managerial staff, and a saving of 630,000 rubles a year effected. The released engineers and technicians found employment in production jobs, without reduction in pay.

The important point about the People's Controllers, says Kovanov, is that they are elected directly by the people to guard the people's interests. They have the duty among others of checking up on the work of the Soviets and their democratic functioning. They are the eyes and the ears of the Soviet people looking after their own interests.

An article in the *Soviets of Working People's Deputies* (December 12, 1967) by Zaluzhny, Vice President of the Committee of People's Control, tells of the relation of the People's Control organization to the local Soviets. First of all, he writes, the organs of People's Control must be considered as the greatest possible help to the Soviets; they mutually strengthen and support each other's work. Since it is also the duty of the Soviet deputies and volunteer workers to check up on the performance of enterprises, it is essential, he writes, that they do not duplicate each other's work. While this sometimes happens, the general and most successful practice is for the organs of People's Control to coordinate their activities with the local Soviets and their Standing Commissions. Frequently they carry out their checking up work jointly, either working in pairs or groups, or dividing up the territory and exchanging data. In any case, all findings of the people's controllers on cases of laxity, negligence or wastefulness in any institution in the area of a given rural Soviet are reported to that Soviet for action.

Answering Citizens' Complaints

ANOTHER example of the concern of the Soviet Government in increasing participation of the people in managing government affairs was a draft decree issued by the Supreme Soviet on April 12, 1968 "On the procedure for Considering the Proposals, Applications and Complaints of Citizens," which also has a direct application to the work of the Soviets.

Letters and complaints to the press, to the Soviets, to all Soviet institutions, have long been a normal feature of Soviet life. Every newspaper has a special department dealing with them. It is obligatory that all matters of substance either be looked into by special members of the newspapers' staff assigned to this, or be turned over to the appropriate department. Likewise every Soviet, at all levels, has a special department to deal with complaints of citizens made in person or by communication. And every kind of enterprise has its complaint box or book.

Many evils have been corrected in this way, both in matters that can be rectified at once and in others which require detailed investigation. At the same time, many instances of unnecessary delay and red tape occur, as noted by *Izvestia,* commenting on the new decree in its issue of April 29. The newspaper repeated an item printed a few days previously which said:

> In order to solve the housing problem of the two families, the Fatarovs and the Titovs, it would have been necessary only to enter 13 words in an application form. It was a simple case, easily solved in this manner in the end. But before this solution was reached, through an outrageous case of red tape, a person of advanced age had to visit various organizations, day in and day out, for an extended period.

The new draft decree stresses the importance of giving legislative force to the democratic rights of Soviet working people to lodge complaints and to have them promptly considered. The decree makes it obligatory to handle complaints and applications within a definite period, to check up on how they are handled. It makes it a legal offense to hold up action by red tape or bureaucracy. The decree proposes that such matters be acted on immediately or within two weeks at most when no special investigation is needed; if further study and verification are required, the necessary measures must be adopted by the enterprise or institution at fault within a month.

Izvestia commented, in an editorial on April 26:

> Every proposal, every application, every complaint should be the subject of the most thorough study possible, for the absolute majority of the Soviet people, apart from exposing shortcomings, also make suggestions on the ways for eliminating them. They go to their local Soviet bodies and make proposals on questions of political, economic and cultural life and improvement of legislation. They generously share their experiences and are unwilling to be reconciled with things that interfere with us. . . . This is one of the forms of genuine participation of the working people in running the state, this is a manifestation of the high political activity of the Soviet people.

THE SOVIET OF THE VILLAGE NOVOZHIVOTINNOYE ON THE DON

by IVAN KOVALKIN, Novosti Correspondent

NOVOZHIVOTINNOYE is a large village on the bank of the river Don, 20 miles or so from the city off Voronenzh. The Regional Soviet rates it as "average." However, there are some interesting points in its history. For example, many years ago Lillian Voynich, author of the famous novel *The Gadfly,* lived for a time in Novozhivotinnoye.

The lands and the inhabitants of Novozhivotinnoye formerly belonged to an old family of the nobility founded in the first half of the 17th century, the Venevitins. The landlord's grand mansion still stands today: it is now occupied by a secondary school for 436 children. The former building of this school was completely demolished by the fascists. A new schoolhouse will soon be built.

Andrey Shingaryov, tsarist Minister of Agriculture, once described Novozhivotinnoye "as a dying village." He wrote: "According to the 1897 census there are 96 homesteads in Novozhivotinnoye, with a population of 664. The only bed linen the inhabitants know are sack-cloth, outer garments, and straw. They have no blankets at all, while feather pillows are rare possessions. The most common bedding is straw . . . A place where the death rate exceeds the birth rate in five out of ten years, where the average annual increase of the population is 3 per 1,000—such a place is only one step from extinction . . . In the 1900-1901 school-year the pupils of the school numbered 14 boys and 6 girls. There are only two small shops with a negligible store of goods and a kopek turnover. . . ."

This was how the ancestors of the contemporary inhabitants of Novozhivotinnoye lived. All these hardships were observed by Lillian Voynich when she came to Novozhivotinnoye in 1887 to teach the children of landlord Venevitinov English and music.

"We are proud of Voynich," the chairman of the Village Soviet Mitrofan Oznobkin told me, "and we consider her to be practically a townswoman of ours. In the school museum the children have set up a special exhibit devoted to her and her books."

We are including this description of a village Soviet, written by a correspondent of Novosti Press Agency, to illustrate the contrast between a typical village of the USSR today and the situation before the Revolution, and also the resurrection that took place after the Nazi invasion.

Oznobkin willingly filled me in on the present situation. Today the Village Soviet is the legislative body of a community comprising five villages—950 homesteads united into a single economy, the "Rossiya" *kolkhoz*. The *kolkhoz* grows grain, sugar beets, and vegetables on an area of 5,600 hectares (one hectare = 2.47 acres). It has large livestock farms and a poultry "factory," and owns 49 tractors, 30 automobiles, and 138 horses.

On the territory covered by the Village Soviet are four schools, a hospital, a pharmacy, work-shops and repair shops, and four stores which in 1967 sold goods amounting to 370 thousand rubles, including 160 TV and radio sets and 25 motorcycles.

The 28 Soviet deputies work in five standing commissions dealing with the following problems: agriculture; public education, culture and health services; communal amenities and road construction; budget, sales, purchases; socialist legality and protection of law and order.

The chairman told me that housing, the basic problem of the village, has been solved. The Village Soviet and its standing commission on communal amenities and road construction played an important role in this.

During World War II the fascists bombed Novozhivotinnoye repeatedly, and fired guns and mortars at it. They never captured it, but the damage was very great. After the Soviet armed forces ousted the enemy from the banks of the Don the inhabitants gradually began returning to their village. The houses that had remained standing were repaired. Others lived in shanties and dugouts.

The village began to come back to life. The *kolkhoz* was gradually restored. But even in 1958, when the villagers had already reestablished their home farms, Novozhivotinnoye was still a dreary-looking place, since every homesteader built haphazardly, with no general plan, using any building materials at hand.

On the initiative of the Village Soviet a general meeting was called in 1958. There was only one question on the agenda: "The radical reconstruction of our community." The secretary of the Village Soviet, forty-year old Yellizaveta Fomina, recalled for me:

"The Chairman addressed the meeting. He said that of course nobody denied that it would be better to live in a more civilized manner amidst beautiful surroundings, and therefore we must rebuild Novozhivotinnoye. He said that today most of us could afford this, and the state will extend long-term loans to any one who could not. He went on to explain that it was impossible for all of us to build simultaneously, and that therefore the standing commission of the Village Soviet, together with the village activists, had investigated all the homes of the farms members, and had decided that the first new houses should be built for families living in rickety structures, or for large families occupying small quarters.

"When the Chairman put the question to a vote a forest of hands was raised in favor of building. We had planned on the construction of 40 to 50 new houses a year, but we built as many as 60, and so within five or six years more than 300 new houses were built. At present there are six streets in our village. We have laid out a park on a five hectare area. The inhabitants have planted their own orchards."

Only a dirt road led from Novozhivotinnoye to the asphalted Voronezh highway. In rainy weather it turned into oozy mud. The distance was a mere four kilometers, but the road because impassable. The Village Soviet received many complaints. The voters demanded that a road be built from the village to the highway, and that a regular bus-line service be set up. The road question was discussed many times at the sittings of the executive committee and the sessions of the Soviet. Finally, a good road was laid down from the village to the highway; now regular buses run between the village and Voronezh four times a day.

Here are several excerpts from the book of records of the village Soviet: "On additional landscaping in a new street of Novozhivotinnoye. On laying out flower-beds in front of the postoffice, department store, foodshop, club, and district hospital."

"On the readiness of the combines, harvesters, tractors, and motorcars for the harvesting season."

"On fulfillment of quotas for State purchases of livestock produce from the population during the first half of the year."

A person moves to Novozhivotinnoye for permanent residence. He has to build a house; for this he needs a piece of land. Here, for example, is an excerpt from the minutes of sitting No. 11, held on June 30, 1967: "Examination of application filed by citizen Nikolay Konoshenko, who wants to build a house. Decision: Konoshenko is granted permission to build a new house on the land between the houses belonging to Alexey Korablin and the two-storeyed building of the *Selkhoztechnika*."

"On the activities of the parent's committee of the secondary school."

"On organization of recreation for schoolchildren during their summer vacation."

"On elimination of explosives from the territory of the Village Soviet." This decision was taken after two boys came to the Soviet and reported that they had discovered a cache of explosives and three caches of projectiles and mines left by the Nazis 24 years ago. The *Ispolkom* immediately got in touch with the nearest military unit. In the last clause of its decision the executive recorded: "Families of farm members residing near the discovered munition caches are to be moved to a safe place for the duration of the soldiers' work." The projectiles and explosives were removed and detonated.

Spring arrived. The snow began to thaw out rapidly. The *Ispolkom* of the Village Soviet planned a meeting devoted to the sanitary state of the communities under its jurisdiction. This meeting was prepared by the standing commission for public education, culture, and health services. The commission invited deputies of the Village Soviet, doctors from the local hospital, and activists in general to attend the meeting. People were assigned to inspect all the communities. Afterwards the commission summed up the data obtained and forwarded the material to the *Ispolkom*. At its meeting the executive heard the reports of the head doctor of the hospital, the doctor's sanitary assistant, and the Chairman of the standing commission.

"We are too liberal with violators of the sanitary rules in the village communities," said deputy Maria Fyodorova, section-leader of the *kolkhoza* Rossiya." "How much longer shall we tolerate the messes in the yards of the consumers' cooperative and around the warehouse of the foodshop? It is time we learned to respect the decisions of the *Ispolkom*. The management of the cooperative must be severely reprimanded."

Many of those present at the meeting criticized the individuals whose fault it was that the streets, farms, warehouses, or private yards were cluttered up and filthy. The *Ispolkom* adopted a resolution requiring the private individuals or organizations who were at fault, to put an end to the unsanitary conditions within one week. The deputies and other responsible persons were charged with checking up on the results. Everything was cleaned up in short order.

Maria Yakovleva is forty years old. She is tall and slender, wears a short sheepskin coat, "valenki" (felt boots), and an angora shawl. Her open face is roughened by the wind, and her blue eyes look cheerfully at the person she is talking with. Maria's husband, Dmitri, is a member of the building team of the Rossiya collective farm. Her aged mother and two sons, Volodya and Alexander, live with them.

It is neat and cozy in their home, a samovar hums busily.

Maria speaks of her production work. She heads a section, the nine members of which cultivate and harvest 13 hectares of sugar beets.

"We have no complaints about earnings," says Maria in conclusion. "We are a well-matched team in regard to work. But we often have arguments and troubles, frequently having nothing to do with our work: family trouble and all other kinds of petty things. The members of my section usually say to me: 'You aren't only our section-head, you're our deputy, too. So go ahead and do something about the matter!' As a deputy of the Soviet I am on the shop committee, and now I have been assigned the job of auditing the papers of the collective farm for 1967."